Neil Simon

Twayne's United States Authors Series

Warren French, Editor
Indiana University, Indianapolis

TUSAS 447

NEIL SIMON
(1927–   )
Photograph courtesy of
DaSilva & DaSilva,
Attorneys at Law

Neil Simon

By Robert K. Johnson

Suffolk University

Twayne Publishers · *Boston*

Neil Simon

Robert K. Johnson

Copyright © 1983 by G.K. Hall & Company
All Rights Reserved
Published by Twayne Publishers
A Division of G. K. Hall & Company
70 Lincoln Street
Boston, Massachusetts 02111

Book Production by Marne B. Sultz

Book Design by Barbara Anderson

**Library of Congress Cataloging in
Publication Data**

Johnson, Robert K.
Neil Simon.

(Twayne's United States authors series;
TUSAS 447)
Bibliography: p. 149
Includes index.
1. Simon, Neil—Criticism and
interpretation.
I. Title. II. Series.
PS3537.I663Z73   1983   812'.54   82-23400
ISBN 0-8057-7387-8

For Warren French

Contents

About the Author

Robert Kenneth Johnson was born in New York City. He attended Queens College, New York University, and Hofstra College, receiving the B.A. in English from Hofstra. Aided by a Woodrow Wilson Fellowship, he was able to obtain the M.A. degree at Cornell University in 1960. Denver University's English Department awarded him a Fellowship; and he concluded the Ph.D. work there in 1963.

He has taught at Loretto Heights College, DePauw University, and the University of Missouri at Kansas City. Since 1968 he has taught in Boston at Suffolk University, where he is a Professor of English. Courses he has offered include Great Books of World Literature, Modern American Poetry, and World on Film.

Interested in writing as well as in teaching, over the years Professor Johnson has had various kinds of original work published, including movie reviews, book reviews, literary criticism, short stories, essays, and poetry. Some of his articles have focused on Robert Frost, William Carlos Williams, Archibald MacLeish, and Howard Nemerov. He is the author of a book for the Twayne Theatrical Arts Series, *Francis Ford Coppola*. Excerpts from that book and from an essay on Richard Wilbur were reprinted in *Contemporary Literary Criticism*. Approximately one hundred of his poems have appeared in various magazines and a collection of his poetry, *Blossoms of the Apricot*, was published in 1975. A second collection, *Passing Moments*, is being prepared for publication.

Preface

I wrote this book primarily because I believe that Neil Simon has not received as much critical attention as he deserves. He is often described as a writer whose plays and filmscripts contain strings of gags recited by one-dimensional characters. Even concerning the weakest efforts by this prolific author, this description is an oversimplification. Concerning the bulk of Simon's writings—to say nothing of his best work—the description is without any validity.

Simon's work *is* funny, and I have noted in the text some of the funny lines, particularly in the early plays. Because Simon's foremost strength as a writer, however, is his ability to present his funny lines through vivid characters and intriguing plot situations, I have focused my attention on a detailed analysis of his plots and characters. Such a scrutiny reveals that most of Simon's characters are not only lifelike, but more complicated and more interesting than most characters populating successful stage and screen comedies. Simon has, in fact, created a rich variety of entertaining, memorable characters who tell us much about the human experience. Simon's work also explores a larger number of serious themes and points of view than he is credited with presenting. Furthermore, he returns to these themes and viewpoints while pushing himself into more difficult and quite varied stylistic formats.

To the best of my knowledge, the only other full-length study of Simon's work is *Neil Simon: A Critical Study* by Edythe M. McGovern. McGovern's book offers many insights, but does not discuss Simon's screenplays, the stage musicals he helped create, or the stage comedies he wrote after *Chapter Two*. In my book, I have focused on everything Simon wrote for the stage and screen starting with *Come Blow Your Horn* and concluding with *Only When I Laugh*. Regarding Simon's film work, I have given little attention to his adaptations of his plays; for—as Simon himself has made clear—these adaptations, with one exception, follow the plays quite closely, and I discuss those plays at length. With Simon's original screenplays, I have as much as possible treated them as I do the texts of the plays. I analyze the screenplay, but avoid any detailed discussion of the acting, direction, etc., unless one of these aspects of the film demands a direct comment.

I did most of my research at two libraries. I want to express my gratitude to Mrs. Vivian D. McIver and her staff at the Needham Public Library and to James Coleman, Mary Florio, and Cathy Axon, staff members of Suffolk University's College of Liberal Arts Library, for all the assistance they gave me. I would also like to thank Dr. Fred Wilkins, Chairman of Suffolk University's English Department, who supported my project in a variety of ways. Finally, I want to offer my special thanks to my wife, Pat, for her help and patience while I worked on my manuscript.

Robert K. Johnson

Suffolk University

Chronology

1927   Born 4 July in New York City, Marvin Neil Simon is the second of two male offspring. His parents were Irving Simon, a garment salesman, and Mamie Simon.

1943–1946   Graduates from De Witt Clinton High School in the Bronx. Enters the Army Air Force Reserve training program at New York University. In August 1945, assigned to Lowry Field, Colorado. Discharged in 1946.

1948–1955   Teams up with his brother, Danny, and writes for the Borscht Circuit and for radio and television shows featuring Robert Q. Lewis, Phil Silvers, Tallulah Bankhead, among others; writes sketches for *Catch a Star!* in 1955 and for *New Faces of 1956*.

1953   Marries Joan Baim. They have two children, Ellen and Nancy. Mrs. Simon died in 1973.

1956–1959   Writes material for "Your Show of Shows," starring Sid Caesar and Imogene Coca, and for comedians Phil Silvers, Garry Moore, and Jerry Lewis; wins an Emmy award in 1957 for his contribution to "The Sid Caesar Show" and in 1959 for the "Sergeant Bilko" series.

1961   *Come Blow Your Horn* (play).

1962   Book for *Little Me* (musical comedy).

1963   *Barefoot in the Park* (play).

1965   *The Odd Couple* (play).

1966   Book for *Sweet Charity* (musical comedy); *The Star-Spangled Girl* (play); *After the Fox* (screenplay).

1967   *Barefoot in the Park* (screenplay).

1968   Book for *Promises, Promises* (musical comedy); *Plaza Suite* (play); *The Odd Couple* (screenplay).

1969   *Last of the Red-Hot Lovers* (play).

1970   *The Gingerbread Lady* (play); *The Out-of-Towners* (screenplay).

1971   *The Prisoner of Second Avenue* (play); *Plaza Suite* (screenplay).

1972   *The Sunshine Boys* (play); *The Heartbreak Kid* (screenplay); *Last of the Red-Hot Lovers* (screenplay).

1973   Marries actress Marsha Mason. *The Good Doctor* (play).

1974   *God's Favorite* (play); *The Sunshine Boys* (screenplay).

1975   *The Prisoner of Second Avenue* (screenplay).

1976   *California Suite* (play); *Murder by Death* (screenplay).

1977   *Chapter Two* (play); *The Goodbye Girl* (screenplay).

1978   *The Cheap Detective* (screenplay).

1979   Book for *They're Playing Our Song* (musical comedy); *California Suite* (screenplay); *Chapter Two* (screenplay).

1980   *I Ought to Be in Pictures* (play); *Seems Like Old Times* (screenplay).

1981   *Fools* (play); *Only When I Laugh* (screenplay).

Chapter One
Broadway Bound

Early Years

Marvin Neil Simon was born in New York City on 4 July 1927. His parents, Irving Simon, a garment salesman, and Mamie Simon, lived first in the Bronx and then in Manhattan. Simon's early years were unhappy ones. He had to live through the traumatic experience of seeing his father walk out on the rest of the family not just once, but several times. Undoubtedly these crises nurtured Simon's strong belief, stressed in many of his plays, in the primary importance of marriage and the family unit.

During the distressing periods when they were abandoned by Simon's father, the rest of the family had to take in lodgers in order to survive economically. Simon sought relief from his unhappiness by going to the movies. He relished the films of Charlie Chaplin, Buster Keaton, and Laurel and Hardy. "I was constantly being dragged out of movies for laughing too loud," Simon later recalled. As a result, his first goal as a playwright was "to make a whole audience fall onto the floor, writhing and laughing so hard that some of them pass out."[1]

While attending De Witt Clinton High School, Simon particularly enjoyed the humor written by Mark Twain, Robert Benchley, and George S. Kaufman. Although he was only an average student, he graduated in 1943 at age sixteen and went to work in the garment district. Many years afterwards, when asked if he did not work himself too hard as a writer, Simon replied, "When I was 16, I worked in the garment district lifting heavy things. Now I just sit at the typewriter and get cookies and milk when I want them."[2]

Although he became an engineering student at New York University while in the Army Air Force Reserve training program, Simon never finished college, something that has caused him to feel inferior at times. He likened his educational limitations to "being in a room where

1

everybody speaks French but you."[3] After a stint at Lowry Field in Colorado, Simon was discharged in 1946. Simon's older brother, Danny, did publicity work for Warner Brothers' New York office, and Simon got a job there in the mail-room. Danny and he had already worked together as a comedy-writing team, fashioning funny patter for a show put on by Abraham and Straus employees. Now, learning that Goodman Ace, a CBS producer and writer, was on the lookout for new comedy writers, the two brothers approached Ace, who asked them to create a comic routine. They were put on the payroll when they devised a Brooklyn usherette's account of a Joan Crawford movie: "She's in love with a gangster who is caught and sent to Sing Sing and given the electric chair and she promises to wait for him."[4]

Simon never looked back. His brother and he were assigned to the Robert Q. Lewis show. In the next four years, they worked for Phil Silvers, Jerry Lester, and Jackie Gleason, among others. They wrote for benefits and for shows put on in the famous Borscht Circuit in resort hotels in the Catskill Mountains. They revised some of this material for the musical review *Catch a Star!* During this time, Simon met and married the dancer Joan Baim. Simon's two offspring, Ellen and Nancy, are from this marriage. Still working together as writers, Neil and Danny Simon created sketches for a Broadway show, *New Faces of 1956,* that became a hit of the season. Then, while Danny settled on the West Coast to pursue his goal of becoming a director, Neil became an outstanding member of the now legendary team of writers devising material for the most famous television comedy weekly of its time, NBC's "Your Show of Shows," starring Sid Caesar and Imogene Coca. Simon later won an Emmy award in 1957 for his contribution to "The Sid Caesar Show" and for "Sergeant Bilko," starring Phil Silvers, in 1959.

Come Blow Your Horn

The pivotal turn in Simon's career occurred when he accepted a five-week assignment for a Jerry Lewis show. Finishing the project ahead of schedule, he started the first draft of *Come Blow Your Horn.* "Having read a lot of books on playwriting," Simon said later, "I knew that you should write about what you know. I figured, OK, I know my family, so I'll do something about how my older brother Danny and I left home and took our first apartment."[5] It took Simon three grueling years to finish the play. Revaluating *Come Blow Your Horn* many years later, Simon wrote that the play, "in the time it was written, seemed like a monumental effort. Today, it seems like the crude markings in a cave by the first prehistoric chronicler."[6] It should be kept in mind, however, that Simon would naturally want the quality of the achievement to equal the intensity of the effort, and that he would be apt to judge any disparity between the two more harshly than it might deserve.

Come Blow Your Horn centers on two brothers, Alan and Buddy Baker. Both work for their father, but only Alan, the older of the two, has his own apartment, where the play takes place. Buddy, treated even more like a baby by his tyrannical father and overindulgent mother than his brother is, asks Alan to let him come live in the apartment. Alan applauds the idea, but Mrs. Baker and then Mr. Baker try unsuccessfully to coerce Buddy into returning home. Instead of capitulating, Buddy begins to imitate and embellish on Alan's freewheeling life-style.

Alan, on the other hand, runs into trouble. Although he has seduced several women, including Peggy Evans, an upstairs neighbor, the woman he is fondest of—Connie Dayton—declares that, before surrendering her virginity to him, she wants Alan to back up his expressions of love for her by marrying her. Finally, she offers him a choice: she will either marry him or move in with him sans wedding ring. Alan opts for the latter alternative—until Connie appears with her suitcases. Then he begrudgingly proposes to her. Hurt by his reluctance, Connie stalks out of the apartment. To add to his woes, Alan is responsible for a mixup in communications that causes a rich customer to desert the family business. Mr. Baker, enraged at Alan's blunder and at Buddy's new carefree behavior, fires both of them.

Alan at first criticizes Buddy, then quickly realizes that it is right for his younger brother to sow his wild oats; but he also realizes it is time for him to stop doing so. He wins Connie back with a more tender proposal of marriage, and he negotiates a lucrative financial deal for the family business, thus gaining his father's blessings.

Once, talking about play structure, Simon stated, "Every scene I write has to have conflict,"[7] a sound principle he utilizes in his first play. The conflict at the beginning of the play results from Peggy's semireluctance to resume the primarily sexual affair that she and Alan embarked on over a weekend. While he is coaxing her, Alan calls her "Connie," as he has done before. By use of this old dramatic ploy, Simon simultaneously indicates that Alan has developed a serious emotional attachment for Connie and that the play, by focusing on Alan's altering character, is going to explore what constitutes a "mature man." This latter point is immediately elaborated upon when Buddy arrives and asks to share

Alan's living quarters. The brothers discuss one major reason for their slowness to mature, namely, their father's refusal to allow them to become a central part of the family business.

Soon afterwards, Mr. Baker appears on the scene, at which point the play—up to now predominantly exposition—shifts into high gear. That Mr. Baker is at least partially to blame for his sons' immaturity is emphasized both by their fear of him and by the insightful comments Alan dares to make. Alan tells his father, "You never ask my advice about the business."[8] When Mr. Baker asserts that if Alan came to work early, his comments would be listened to, Alan retorts, "I did. For three years. Only then I was 'too young' to have anything to say. And now that I've got my own apartment, I'm too much of a 'bum' to have anything to say. Admit it, Dad. You don't give me the same respect you give the night watchman" (29).

In a scene between the brothers, Alan tells Buddy to grow up and be "a man." At this point, Alan means simply that Buddy should become a playboy like himself. What the play proceeds to demonstrate is that Simon's definition of "a man" is more complicated than Alan's. For Simon, a man is someone who asserts his independence and experiments with a variety of life's offerings, but who ultimately does not ignore the traditionally richest human experiences founded on love, marriage, and family. Alan gradually comprehends that his playboy life has ceased to nurture his maturity and has become, instead, a means of his avoiding maturing any further.

Feisty, but basically conventional, Connie pressures Alan to examine his current mode of living. Tired of her own rootless life, and sincerely in love with Alan, she has resolved to forsake a show-business career and settle down—with Alan, if possible. Alan procrastinates; yet the depth of his feeling for Connie is dramatized when, finding Connie ready to live with him even though he will not marry her, he backs away from this offer. It is unlikely that such an arrangement, if contemplated by two young people living later in the 1960s, would trigger so much anxiety; nor would there necessarily be so much importance placed on Connie's virginity. But both Alan and Connie still embody an early post–World War II point of view.

In typical light-comedy fashion, all the problems in the play are resolved in the third act. Buddy, improvising a life-style that foreshadows the next decade's "swinging singles" world, shocks Alan into a full awareness that Alan's basic values are quite conservative, and that it is time for Alan to honor those values in his private life. Alan and his father also come to terms with one another. The audience has learned earlier that, despite his bluster, Mr. Baker has been terribly shaken by Alan's leaving home and is even more upset by this newest round of rebellion on the part of both offspring. Now Mr. Baker agrees to delegate genuine responsibilities to his sons.

That Simon upholds the concept of the family unit is demonstrated in his implied approval of the fact that—despite their parents' attempts to control them and despite Mr. Baker's particularly overbearing nature—Alan and Buddy do not at any time want to break off relations with their mother and father completely. Mr. Baker's tyranny is so powerful that even when the boys are living in their own apartment, they are very conscious of their father's influence on their lives. At times, such as when Mr. Baker threatens them with physical punishment, he is almost not "a funny character" in a comedy. Even so, the boys still want to create a healthier, less stifling relationship with their parents and to win their father's approval.

Simon can be praised for preparing the audience for the basic changes occurring in Alan, Buddy, and their father. Alan's slip-of-the-tongue reference to Connie when he talks with Peggy is the first of several indications of his love for Connie, indications which neatly pave the way for his final marriage proposal. Early in the play, when Mrs. Baker attempts to force Buddy to return home, Buddy insists on dealing with her himself instead of letting Alan do so. This symbolizes Buddy's growing ability to manage his own life. Simon's early stress on Mr. Baker's being upset with his rebellious sons is an even more important contribution to the plausibility of the third act's happy ending, when Mr. Baker yields some of his patriarchal powers. For, because Mr. Baker is the most vivid character in the play, the audience would not be willing to let Simon manipulate Mr. Baker in any way Simon wanted to.

Although the four main characters in the play are based on Simon's parents, his brother, Danny, and Simon himself, the reason Mr. Baker is the most interesting of the four is that Simon moved closer to the living model than he did when creating Mrs. Baker and the two sons, who are simpler—and flatter—stereotypes. Mrs. Baker is, in fact, only a moderately amusing variation of the "Jewish Mother," and almost entirely peripheral to the conflicts that take place. Simon salvages something on her behalf by giving her a comic telephone routine that, although funny, is contrived and largely inconsequential to the plot.

The play has other weaknesses. The structure is flawed by Simon's bad habit of bringing people, such as Mr. and Mrs. Baker and Connie, back on stage unjustifiably often. When they reappear, they simply go over plot-ground thoroughly gone over already. Other flaws that are comparatively minor in this play, but which recur in later plays, are Simon's fondness for running gags and for what can be described as "the circular joke." An example of the first is the recurring dubious reaction of people who phone Alan and find themselves talking to a female voice that claims to belong to (and does belong to) Alan's mother. Still more belabored is Simon's insistence that the person who rings the doorbell to Alan's apartment not turn out to be the person expected. One typically strained "circular joke" occurs when Buddy urges Alan to phone and find out what has become of Connie after she stalks out of the apartment. The exchange continues:

Alan: What for? I'm not interested. . . . Besides . . . she checked out of her hotel.
Buddy: Oh! Where'd she go?
Alan: How should I know. I didn't ask them.
Buddy: Maybe she left a forwarding address.
Alan: There's no forwarding address.
Buddy: How do you know?
Alan: I asked them. (80)

Nevertheless, *Come Blow Your Horn* is a successful piece of work. Most of the characters are amusing, and one character, Mr. Baker, is a completely fascinating—although in some ways awful—person. The situations are entertaining, and there is an abundance of funny lines. Two lines help prove this last point and, at the same time, show that even in this, his first play, Simon integrated most of his one-liners into the dramatic situation. Buddy proves how oppressively sheltered his life has been—and how much he wants to become a sophisticate—when Alan asks him what he would like to drink. Buddy says he would like a Scotch and ginger ale. Alan comments, "They must know you in every bar in town" (21).

Mr. Baker's ability to intimidate and squelch his sons is also demonstrated early in the play when Alan quaveringly promises to stop being so cavalier about the family business and to "be in the office first thing in the morning." Mr. Baker asks, "You know the address, don't you?" (26).

Finally, *Come Blow Your Horn* contains what becomes another recurring feature in Simon's plays. Although the Baker family's attitudes, speech patterns, and outlook on life are Jewish, Simon refused to specify them as Jews. Apparently in order to make it easier for every member of his theater audience to identify with his characters, Simon continued to shy away from portraying specifically Jewish characters. Occasionally, this vagueness concerning a character's religious beliefs, foreign roots, and cultural heritage diluted the vitality—indeed, the very reality—of that character. Often, however, Simon overcame this problem by creating an inclusive "urban type," a character whose manner of speaking and acting represented both urban Jews and urban Gentiles. Simon also offset the vagueness concerning certain aspects of his characters' backgrounds by presenting other facets of their lives in vivid realistic detail. In *Come Blow Your Horn,* except to some extent for Mr. Baker, thinness of character prevails. Consequently, this comedy's success results from Simon's putting the play's tissue-thin characters in a variety of lively comic situations.

Little Me

Although his income from *Come Blow Your Horn* was less than what he had made as a top television writer, Simon now considered himself a playwright. The next project he completed was the book for *Little Me,* a musical based on Patrick Dennis's novel featuring a heroine with a very active lovelife. Simon was taken aback by the prospect of a show starring seven leading men. Then he conceived the idea of having Sid Caesar enact all seven parts.

The crux of the plot, related by the heroine in her old age, is spelled out in its third scene. Buxom but poor Belle Schlumpfert and wealthy Noble Eggleston, a definitely straight-arrow young man, fall in love. Mrs. Eggleston, domineering and snobbish, keeps the two apart by demanding that Belle attain wealth, culture, and social position before the lovers be allowed to marry. Belle gains some money by melting the cold heart of rich old Mr. Pinchley. Unfortunately, she accidentally causes Pinchley to shoot and kill himself. Noble saves Belle from the death penalty, but when she learns that Noble has been pressured into marrying well-to-do Ramona, she attempts suicide.

She is saved by Val du Val, a nightclub entertainer, and is comforted so ardently by longtime friend George Musgrove that she becomes pregnant. She marries a naive soldier, Fred Poitrine, who dies of a self-inflicted wound sustained while typing a letter to the Quartermaster. She then loyally marries Val du Val in order to save him from a nervous breakdown. The ship they are on sinks; Val drowns, and Belle, by suing the steamship company, gains a fortune. She achieves cultural distinc-

tion by bankrolling a movie studio's production of an artistically successful film that leads to the death of its egotistical director, Otto Schnitzler.
When she financially rescues the kingdom of Rosenzweig, its Prince
makes her a countess—before he dies from another accident perpetrated
by Belle.

Because Belle has achieved all three of her goals, and because the
marriage between Noble and Ramona has been annulled, Belle and Noble
marry. Their troubles are still not over, however. Belle introduces Noble to
hard liquor. He becomes an alcoholic and deserts her, and she marries
George. Just as Mrs. Eggleston attempts to shoot Belle, Noble, now
reformed, returns. The gun, fought over by Mrs. Eggleston and Belle,
goes off. George is fatally wounded; and Belle and Noble are reunited one
final time.

The play offered the audience many good things, including Carolyn
Leigh's clever lyrics and the choreography by young Bob Fosse. The
major reason for the show's long run, though, was the performance of Sid
Caesar, particularly in the roles of Pinchley, Schnitzler, and the Prince.
When Pinchley's son suggests that they, as bank owners, show the poor
people a little mercy, Pinchley tries to swat his son with a cane and
shouts, "This is a bank, son, not a mother!"[9] In creating the characters of
Schnitzler and the Prince, Simon elaborated on roles Caesar had already
explored on his television shows. Prussian-like Schnitzler, a take off on
director Erich von Stroheim, claims to have been humbled by having
made twelve rotten pictures in a row. Nonetheless, when Belle permits
him to direct another picture and tells him she will join him on the set
the next morning at eight o'clock, Schnitzler places a monocle in his eye
and replies, "You'll be there at six and if you're late, you're fired" (111).
The Prince is a semiaddlepated, stereotyped Pole. He tries to solve his
country's woeful financial problems by betting all its remaining wealth
on one turn of the roulette wheel. When he loses, he whips out a gun.
His friends plead with him not to commit suicide. He points the gun at
the casino director and says, "This is a stickup" (125).

Yet, even in its best segments, *Little Me* fails to utilize fully its richest
material. Other segments never get off the ground. The fundamental
problem is that the play has no cohesive point of view. The play begins by
stressing that Belle's autobiography will tell the truth—"dates, places,
vivid descriptions" (15). Simon's script, however, reveals no startling or
sardonic truths. If the musical were meant to burlesque success stories
written by aging celebrities, it fails because Belle's career is too fragmented and is often overshadowed by the male characters Caesar played.

At times, Belle seems to represent a comic femme fatale who gains her goals by proving fatal, albeit unintentionally, to the men in her life. Yet she does not even indirectly cause the death of Poitrine and Val du Val. Belle turns out to be simply a character who loosely ties together a series of humorous sketches.

Several satiric possibilities are wasted or wandered away from. When Noble and his snooty friends happen on the "slum" Belle first lives in, Noble comes up with the charitable idea of giving some of their picnic food to the poor. He naively explains that this is "the democratic way. Eat until you think you're gonna bust, and then give away the leftovers" (22). But this rather harmless political "thrust" is not the forerunner of any deeper political humor. The satiric potential regarding nasty Pinchley is abandoned when Pinchley, scolded by Belle, immediately does a complete about-face and becomes Mr. Generous. As Howard Taubman observed, "What a loss in satirical impact [occurs] when the antique villain is regenerated so hastily and capriciously."[10] The long sequence in which Belle visits a military hospital during World War I offered Simon ample opportunity for all kinds of humor. One just has to remember what Caesar did in his monologue on war movies in *Tars and Spars.* In *Little Me,* the opportunity is ignored; the hospital scene merely adds a few innocuous plot twists to the story and then fades away.

Actually, Simon had more to say in *Come Blow Your Horn* than in *Little Me.* He apparently had only one specific goal in mind regarding this musical: to provide a theater counterpart to the uncontroversially entertaining routines presented in Caesar's television programs. If so, he achieved his goal.

Barefoot in the Park

Shortly after he started writing *Barefoot in the Park,* Simon began to lose his enthusiasm for the project. He showed the script to producer Saint Subber, who liked the material so much that Simon resumed writing the play. The comedy was an instant hit.

Barefoot in the Park revolves around Corie and Paul Bratter, who have just moved into a New York apartment after a week's honeymoon. Eager to have the honeymoon mood pervade the rest of their married lives, Corie tries to convince Paul, a lawyer, to forget about his job the moment he comes home from the office. Badgered by Corie, Paul turns grumpy. His grouchiness doubles when he learns that Corie is trying to "put romance" into her widowed mother's life by arranging a blind date for her with Victor Velasco, another tenant in the building.

On the night Corie, Paul, Velasco, and Ethel Banks, Corie's mother, go out together, Mrs. Banks tries to be accommodating despite her fatigue and upset stomach. Paul, on the other hand, becomes increasingly sour, so much so that after Mrs. Banks and Velasco start out for Mrs. Banks's home in New Jersey, Corie and Paul argue heatedly. Tired, tipsy, and angry, they discuss getting a divorce. The next day, stung by Corie's criticisms, Paul—to prove he is not changing into an old fuddy-duddy—eventually gets drunk, walks barefoot in the park even though it is the dead of winter, and climbs onto the apartment building's roof, from which Corie has to rescue him. In the meantime, learning that her mother passed out and had to spend the night in Velasco's rooms, Corie regrets instigating the previous night's party.

All works out well in the end. Ethel Banks feels her physical troubles are inconsequential compared to her having had one of the most exciting nights in her life. She is glad to end her lonely widow's existence. Velasco acknowledges that he is too old for late-night carousing and becomes genuinely interested in Mrs. Banks. Corie and Paul recognize the worth of the traits they have in common and the traits that only the other possesses.

As the play begins, Simon stresses two points. One is Corie's personality. After the telephone man installs a phone, Corie's romantic nature is defined when she waxes ecstatic over "Eldorado five, eight, one, nine, one"[11]—her new phone number. Previous to this, Corie enters the apartment with a bouquet of flowers, the "first bit of color in the room" (106), after almost effortlessly climbing a stoop plus five flights of stairs. The great number of steps leading up to the apartment is the other point stressed.

Edythe M. McGovern praises the play for making "little use"[12] of running gags, a device employed all too frequently in *Come Blow Your Horn*. This is curious praise, for perhaps Simon's single most famous running gag occurs in *Barefoot in the Park*, a gag centered on those six sets of steps. At times the gag is quite effective. For one thing, it provides the play with several funny lines. For another, it helps define the individual characters by inviting the audience to compare these characters' reactions to climbing all those steps. Corie's reaction emphasizes her exuberance and good humor. Velasco's desire to "think young" is revealed when he ignores the physical problem of the steps. That Mrs. Banks is a good sport is established by her determination not to make a big thing over her being momentarily drained of energy by the climb. On the other hand, Paul's tendency toward grumpiness is emphasized when he harps on how tiring the climb is.

In his review, John McCarten insisted that the gag is unrealistic because Simon foolishly underestimated "the hardihood of the average walkup dweller."[13] McCarten missed the point—and not simply because he forgot that in the context of the plot only Velasco qualifies as an "average walkup dweller." With regard to Corie and Paul, the important point is that the climb affects them to the degree they let it affect them. McCarten's irritation with the running gag, however, is justified. It is milked too dry. We are not only given the lengthy initial reactions of Paul and Mrs. Banks to the climb, we are given in Act Two their lengthy second reactions, and, in Paul's case, third reaction. We are also given the reactions of the telephone man—twice—and the delivery man.

Another flaw in the play involves Corie's relationship with her mother. At first Corie is very apprehensive about her mother's opinions. When she tells the telephone man that the many flights of stairs will discourage people from visiting Paul and herself, he asks her what specific people she means; she replies, "Mothers, friends, relatives, mothers" (108). Afraid that her mother will disapprove of the apartment, Corie pressures Paul into agreeing to lie about how much rent they are paying. Even when Mrs. Banks repeatedly assures Corie that she likes the apartment, Corie insists that she knows her mother actually hates it. Only when Paul leaves the two women alone and Mrs. Banks kisses Corie and praises the rooms still more does Corie allow herself to believe that her mother likes the place. She explains her apprehension by stating that choosing the apartment is the "first thing I've ever done on my own" (131). Yet after all this evidence that Corie is as nervous about parental approval as Alan and Buddy Baker were in *Come Blow Your Horn,* Corie is never again concerned about her mother's endorsement of anything. In fact, she begins to run her mother's life. In Act Three, when she asks her mother for help in coping with Paul, Mrs. Banks exclaims, "That's the first time you've asked my advice since you were ten" (207), an almost direct contradiction of Corie's remark about not doing things on her own.

Fortunately, this abrupt reversal in the women's relationship occurs amid some of the best fun in the play. Mrs. Banks's reactions to the apartment are very amusing—especially her repeated quick switches from puzzlement to emphatic approval. Mrs. Banks, for instance, exclaims that the bedroom is so small that there is no way to get by the bed and to the closet. When Corie asserts that there is, her mother asks, "Without climbing over the bed?" Corie says, "No, you *have* to climb over the bed." Without missing a beat, Mrs. Banks replies, "That's a good idea" (128). These rapid reversals highlight Mrs. Banks's single most important characteristic: she is a good sport. So, too, the reason prompting Corie's shift in attitude toward her mother subsumes the audience's surprise at the suddenness of the shift. Corie's wish that her mother stop living alone and fall in love again derives from a change in Corie that is central to the whole play. She tells her mother that her honeymoon week was "wonderful," that she found "spiritual, emotional, and physical love" (134).

Corie's new awareness of the sexual happiness marriage can bring is the core of her dismay when Paul becomes less interested in love-making. Apparently, like Alan Baker's sweetheart Connie, Corie was a virgin up to her wedding day. Only during her honeymoon did she experience the pleasures of total sexual fulfillment. Now she rates physical love as at least as important as spiritual and emotional love. Corie's intense sexual nature has been fully aroused. After Paul goes to the office, she dons the clothes he has taken off precisely because they have just been next to his flesh. She cannot bear the thought of seeing the sexual element of their marriage dwindle in importance to Paul as he becomes preoccupied with his job. Hence her "overreaction" to Paul's decision to spend an evening preparing for his appearance in court the next day. At night, she tells him, she wants him "to be here and sexy" (117).

The play's tug-of-war between Corie and Paul results also from Corie's still somewhat shaky perception of Paul's basic personality. This is underscored by the differing views of Paul that Corie and her mother have. Corie, speaking to Paul early in the play about her mother, asserts, "She has a different set of values. She's practical. She's not young like us" (123). Later, Mrs. Banks says to Corie, "I worry about you two. You're so impulsive. You jump into life. Paul is like me. He looks first" (131). At this time Corie tends to agree with her mother's description.

The audience, on the other hand, realizes the differences in the personalities of Corie and Paul the moment Paul enters the apartment. Paul is so intimidated by all those flights of stairs that he staggers through the doorway. He clutches his attaché case, which represents the orderly world of the law—a world he enjoys and succeeds in. Informed that his first court case will come up the next morning, he is delighted—and is taken aback that Corie is displeased he has promised a law partner to review all the pertinent material that night. Unlike Corie, he is upset, not intrigued, to find out that several oddballs, including Victor Velasco, reside in their building. Simon's only weak character delineation in the play is Velasco. He is an all too familiar type: the middle-aged charmer with a foreign air about him and a semi-Bohemian attitude who gaily defies all mundane matters, including paying the rent. Simon creates little that is new in his version of this type. What makes Velasco's cliché character stand out all the more is that he is juxtaposed to Mrs. Banks, a character even more interesting than Paul and Corie. Mrs. Banks is straightforward, yet tactful. She is slow on the uptake, yet quickwitted. She is set in her ways, yet flexible. She is afraid, yet adventurous; independent, yet lonely. She does not want to accept dares, yet she does risk much. She is humiliated, yet undaunted. In sum, she encompasses a wide range of thoughts, feelings, and attitudes.

The two-scene second act, featuring "the night on the town" for the newlyweds, Mrs. Banks, and Velasco, builds in hilarity, a hilarity framed by Paul's early-evening comment to Corie, "This thing tonight has 'fiasco' written all over it" (148). Velasco insists on dictating the major decisions, which lead the foursome to an Albanian restaurant on Staten Island. When Velasco departs later that night, presumably to escort Mrs. Banks to her New Jersey home, the tension building all week between Corie and Paul peaks. Aware that Velasco has no ready means of transportation for returning from New Jersey at that hour of the night, Corie has her first misgivings about the date she has set up. That is all the opening Paul needs in order to criticize her as irresponsible. She responds by accusing him of being a timid "Watcher" instead of a "Do-er" (175). Her final accusation is, "You wouldn't walk barefoot with me in Washington Square Park." When Paul defends his refusal by reminding her it was only seventeen degrees above zero, Corie shouts, "Exactly. That's very sensible and logical. Except it isn't any fun" (177). Because both of them are dead tired, more than a little drunk, and employing a screwball logic, they discuss getting a divorce. Paul accuses Corie of lacking common sense and emotional maturity. She says simply that they have nothing in common.

In his determination to bring about a happy ending for his comedy, Simon overmanipulates his characters in the third act, which takes place the next day. First, straining to wring more laughs out of their tiff and to make their reconciliation all the sweeter, Simon has his newlyweds remain determined to get a divorce, even though it is highly unlikely that, cold sober, they would still be that silly. Simon starts to bring the lovers back together again not in a commonsensical way, but via a phonecall from an Aunt Harriet, who informs Corie that her mother never returned home. When Mrs. Banks comes downstairs from Velasco's living quarters, she explains that she became so ill the previous night, she fainted. Velasco injured his foot trying to help her, and both of them had to be carried up to Velasco's apartment. It is hard to believe that Corie and Paul would have remained oblivious to all this commotion right outside their apartment door.

Simon's manipulation shows itself in two other ways. That Mrs. Banks feels all the more chipper after her night's adventure is a bit facile. There is, for instance, the matter of her having slept without a board for her back, yet feeling the better for having done so. A person who needs to sleep on a board would not be in better physical shape after sleeping without it. Simon employs here a weak variation on the old movie cliché in which a character who, although having worn glasses for years, discovers after the glasses are smashed that he sees just fine without them. Also, Corie now believes she had acted as irresponsibly as Paul accused her of acting. She says, "Paul was right. He was right about so many things" (200). When Paul, who had left the apartment with his attaché case and a bottle of liquor, returns dead drunk and begins to act in a wild and woolly way, the contrite Corie declares that she wants the old Paul back. "He's dependable and he's strong and he takes care of me and tells me how much I can spend and protects me" (212). Simon is so intent on making Corie contrite—thus, ready to be lovey-dovey with Paul again—he refuses to permit Corie to perceive even dimly that her scheme on her mother's behalf was not so reckless after all. Her mother comes out of her evening affair having gained the attention of the most interesting man she has met in many years. The blind date was, in fact, a rousing success.

Yet the play easily surmounts these flaws. It does so mainly because of the continued high quality of the humor. What helps, too, is the play's pervading cohesive point of view, which posits the belief that moderation is a primary virtue. Corie's basically romantic nature is fine—as long as she does not insist on it entirely. Paul is not wrong to stress common sense—as long as he does not let it smother all spontaneity, all the quick joy of life. Corie has to realize that the honeymoon cannot last forever. Paul has to realize that there is nothing wrong in continuing to nurture a honeymoon's atmosphere to *some* degree during the weeks, months, and years following the honeymoon.

The practical and the romantic should work in tandem. Paul strolls through the park with his attaché case in one hand and a bottle of liquor in the other, and comes home a nicer human being. Mrs. Banks returns to her daughter's apartment wearing Velasco's bathrobe, but carrying her pocketbook. She, too, is now a still better person. The attaché case and the pocketbook can symbolize the practical side of life, the liquor bottle and the borrowed bathrobe, the romantic side of people's nature. If Corie's reformation is too mechanical, it is not hopelessly so. Her last speeches make it clear that Paul's more mature nature had never been completely unappealing to her. So, too, there were clear early indications that Paul has a zany side to his personality. He keeps his ties neat by pressing them between the pages of a book. He suggests to Corie that they should spend an evening wallpapering each other.

Corie, Paul, and Mrs. Banks all move toward a life-style featuring moderation. So does Velasco. He becomes somewhat more interesting as a character when he reveals that he was deliberately playing the role of the young-at-heart, middle-aged Bohemian. He ruefully admits he has played the role too ardently and too long. He will, perhaps, stop dyeing his hair and eating exotic food by the plateful. While Mrs. Banks will become more carefree, Velasco will become more conservative. Edythe M. McGovern succinctly summed the matter up by stating, "In a very real sense each of the four characters has altered his behavior so that it has become less polarized, less radical, less extreme. Each person has gravitated toward a moderation which seems to be the playwright's ideal."[14]

Simon, however, does not suggest that everybody should have the same portions of practicality, idealism, soberness, romanticism, etc. What is most interesting about Corie and Paul is that they dramatize how one human being provides another with ballast. Although they do reawaken dormant facets of each other's natures that match their own dominant traits, Corie and Paul will never be—or want to be—facsimiles of each other. Nor will Velasco and Mrs. Banks become twins in their traits. In the final analysis, Simon does not want people to duplicate each other, but to complement each other.

In this and other plays, Simon celebrates compromise, rather than insisting a position be maintained in all its stark purity. Because this outlook is a traditional one, some people fail to see that it very neatly binds funny lines and funny characters together. These people conclude that Simon offers no distinguishable point of view in his "cotton candy comedies." Nonetheless, although Simon's viewpoint is an old and conservative one, it remains also a distinct and viable one.

Chapter Two
The Odd Couple

It is significant that Simon originally envisioned *The Odd Couple* as "a black comedy."[1] He wanted to push beyond the simple comedy formats of *Come Blow Your Horn* and *Barefoot in the Park*. The tryout troubles that the new play incurred are also significant. On the first day of rehearsals, Simon realized that he had a weak third act. He began revising it that day and continued altering it throughout the long tryout period.

The play opens with a poker game held at Oscar Madison's apartment, the setting for all the scenes. Felix Ungar is late joining his friends, for earlier in the day his wife and he separated. Oscar, divorced from his wife, Blanche, offers to let Felix move in with him, and Felix accepts the invitation. The two men, however, immediately begin to get on each other's nerves. Oscar is lazy, disorganized, and sloppy. Felix is compulsively neat and a hypochondriac.

During another poker game two weeks later, the friction between the two men intensifies. A few nights later, Oscar arranges a double-date for Felix and himself with Cecily and Gwen Pigeon. On that evening, Oscar upsets Felix by thoughtlessly causing the meal Felix has cooked to burn up. Felix spoils everyone else's mood by delivering a morose monologue about his separation from his wife and two children. The next evening Oscar, still fuming, tells Felix to move out of the apartment, and Felix does so. But it is clear to Oscar's poker-playing cronies, back for another game, that Oscar feels guilty about throwing Felix out into the night. Then Felix returns with the Pigeon sisters to collect the rest of his things; the two women, taking pity on Felix, have invited him to share their quarters. Oscar is surprised, but relieved, and the two men part amicably.

Simon skillfully makes the weekly poker games an entertaining means of presenting expository information about Oscar and Felix and highlighting the domestic changes in the two men's lives. Simon underscores those changes by contrasting them with the sameness of the poker-game format. During the game in Act One, for instance, the audience quickly learns that Oscar is more than a bit of a slob. He offers his friends "brown sandwiches and green sandwiches." When asked what the green is, he replies, "It's either very new cheese or very old meat." One friend, Roy, commenting on Oscar's housecleaning inabilities, observes, "His refrigerator's been broken for two weeks. I saw milk standing in there that wasn't even in the bottle."[2] Even though Oscar is a highly paid sportswriter, he owes the other players money. Through a phonecall from his ex-wife, the audience discovers he is three or four weeks behind in alimony payments. Because it is unusual for Felix to be late for the game, the other men worry aloud about him. By this means, Simon sketches in much of Felix's basic personality. Particular emphasis is placed on his hypochondria and other fears and on his compulsive desire for neatness.

After the other men leave, Oscar and Felix elaborate on their own personalities, particularly their faults. Felix speaks of coming home after his wife and the hired help had cleaned all the rooms and cleaning the rooms again himself. A good cook, he recooked all the meals. Oscar describes some of his own marital faults. He let his cigars burn holes in the furniture and he drank too much. He insensitively dragged his wife to a hockey game to "celebrate" their tenth wedding anniversary.

Still, the two men reveal more about themselves to the audience than they do to each other. Oscar, for instance, is not wholly the happy-go-lucky guy he appears to be. He humorously admits to his friends that he loves to bluff while playing poker. It becomes evident, however, that he puts up a front in other ways, too. Although he seems unconcerned about living alone, he tells Felix, "When you walk into eight empty rooms every night it hits you in the face like a wet glove" (244). When Felix remains hesitant about moving in, Oscar blurts out that he truly wants Felix to move in, and that he is not just doing Felix a favor. He says, "I can't stand living alone" (248).

Felix, too, gives himself away more than he realizes when he declares himself a better cook and, by implication, a better financial manager and housecleaner than his wife, Frances. He is so intent on listing his faults he fails to perceive that he is, in fact, almost entirely absorbed in himself. Unlike the audience, Felix is startled when told he is full of self-love, an observation Oscar makes when he states he has "never *seen* anyone so in love" (246) with himself as Felix is. This same shoe, however, also fits Oscar's foot. Oscar says he is impossible to live with; but he does not really believe this is so—else he would not invite Felix to come live with him.

In point of fact, for all the self-criticism the two engage in, neither man truly thinks he is such a bad guy. Each is tacitly convinced his good qualities far outweigh his faults. Moreover, each believes that some of the faults confessed to are actually either not faults at all or are faults bred and subsumed by virtues. Deep down in their hearts, both men believe they are by no means entirely to blame for the demise of their marriages. Coming full circle, Oscar asserts, "It takes two to make a rotten marriage" (246). Although not conscious of what they are doing, they think they now, by creating a happy "marriage," are about to prove how decisively their good points eclipse their bad points.

They do not, however, live happily ever after. The first indications of trouble are the direct comments they exchange at the poker game in Act Two. Cleverly, Simon counterpoints the friction between Oscar and Felix by means of the other four participants in the card game. Vinnie and Murray, similar to Felix in temperament, appreciate the changes Felix has rendered in the apartment. They relish especially the striking improvement in the quality of the food offered. Speed and Roy, akin to Oscar in personality, are irritated by the innovations. Roy goes so far as to say he preferred things the way they were before Felix moved in. Felix's self-love prevents him from discerning how annoying his house-keeper's quirks are. Finally sensing Oscar's mounting anger, he says in surprise, "I didn't realize I irritated you that much" (259).

The double-date ignites the final blowup. Before the big evening begins, Felix tells Oscar he will cook the dinner for the foursome; he also promises not to dwell on his unhappy past. Elated, Oscar exclaims, "That's the new Felix I've been waiting for" (266). Oscar's high hopes for the get-together, however, prove unfounded. Almost as soon as he leaves Felix alone with the two women in order to make everyone a drink, Felix breaks his promise. Because he obviously thrives on brooding about his woes, he tells the women how lonely and unhappy he is away from his wife and children. As he verbalizes his feelings for the first extended time since the end of his marriage, the full weight of his sad situation hits him—so much so he breaks down and begins crying. The Pigeon sisters, touched by Felix's sorrow, become teary themselves. Returning to the "party," Oscar finds three very somber people and becomes incensed at Felix. In order to hurt Felix, Oscar informs him that his London broil is ruined.

The whole matter of the food for dinner makes it clear that Felix is not the only one of the two men who continues to display unpleasant, annoying traits. One reason the meat is spoiled is that Oscar promised to be home at seven o'clock and then did not arrive home until eight—

without bothering to inform Felix he would be late. Nonetheless, it still would have been possible for Felix to serve a succulent dinner if it had been served right away, as Felix had wanted it to be. But Oscar insists that they all have a drink first. To top it all off, while he is out in the kitchen mixing drinks, Oscar neglects to check on the London broil. In sum, Oscar is as uncaring as Felix is overly fussy.

When Felix's anger prompts him to declare he will not join Oscar and the ladies in the latters' apartment for the rest of the evening, Oscar says, "You mean you're not going to make any effort to change? This is the person you're going to be—until the day you die?" Felix responds with, "We are what we are" (284). In point of fact, neither man wants to change or thinks he should.

Despite the revisions Simon fashioned during the play's tryout run, the third act dips below the high quality of the preceding acts. Simon himself wrote that *The Odd Couple* is basically a sound play, but that the "seams show a bit in the third act. I rewrote it five times out of town. I think I needed one more town."[3] Because Simon is a master of the rewrite, it is entirely possible that, if allowed more time, he would have made his third act as fine a piece of work as the first two acts are. Even in its present form, the third act deserves praise.

The two men's final confrontation is thoroughly gripping. It is also quite funny. Oscar tries to bully Felix by declaring that everything in the apartment is his own; he concludes, "The only thing here that's yours is you" (286). Felix will not be intimidated. He reminds Oscar that he pays half the rent and then rattles Oscar by threatening to walk around in Oscar's bedroom. Oscar counters by commanding Felix to remove the plate of spaghetti from the poker table. When Felix needles Oscar for not recognizing that the food is linguini, not spaghetti, Oscar hurls the plate against the kitchen wall and states, "Now it's garbage!" (287).

Their confrontation peaks as Felix asks Oscar to be less vague regarding what it is about Felix that bothers him. Felix inquires, "What is it, the cooking? The cleaning? The crying?" Oscar answers, "It's the cooking, cleaning and crying" (288). Felix unloads on Oscar, describing him as "one of the biggest slobs in the world" as well as unreliable and irresponsible. Not to be outdone, Oscar states that he was merely a little dejected after living alone in the apartment for six months, but that now, after living with Felix for only three weeks, "I am about to have a nervous breakdown" (290).

Simon, however, did not wish the play to end with the two men angrily going their separate ways. He wanted a happy ending, an ending that left the audience still tickled by and fond of Felix and Oscar. To achieve this, Simon decided to have the two men part amicably, respecting each other as much or more than they did before they roomed together. Like the characters themselves, the audience is to believe that as a result of their living together, Oscar and Felix have had a positive effect on each other.

In an effort to create a change in Felix's character, Simon has Felix come out of his shell a little and release some of his long-suppressed anger and frustration. Oscar is so surprised by Felix's comparatively uninhibited behavior that he remarks, "What's this? A display of temper?" (289). When Felix believes his wife, Frances, has phoned the apartment, he instructs Murray, who answered the phone, to tell Frances that he "is not the same man she kicked out three weeks ago" (300). Simon indicates that Oscar has changed, too. Although Oscar suppressed whatever modicum of guilt he felt for causing his marriage to end in divorce, he now admits to feeling guilty about throwing Felix out of the apartment. A further indication of his change in personality, and an indication of Felix's effect on him, occurs at the very end of the play. Oscar—for the first time ever—reprimands the other poker players for their sloppiness. He protests, "Watch your cigarettes, will you? This is my house, not a pig sty" (301). Furthermore, both men acknowledge that they have helped each other. Oscar says that Felix should thank him for doing two things—taking Felix in and throwing him out. Felix responds, "You're right, Oscar. Thanks a lot" (299).

All the same, Simon's attempt to create a happy ending for a play that started out as "a black comedy" does not work. By the time he wrote this play, Simon had become too skillful at presenting realistic characters for him suddenly to reduce Oscar and Felix in the third act to puppets he could pull any way he wanted to. When he wrote *Come Blow Your Horn,* he could arrange his happy ending without a great deal of difficulty because, except for Mr. Baker, the characters were little more than slickly depicted, broad types. In *Barefoot in the Park,* Simon produced much more lifelike characters, particularly in Paul, Corie, and, most of all, Mrs. Banks. Consequently, it was harder for Simon to make the characters do whatever he wanted them to do in order to end the play on a cheery note. Hence the partially flawed resolution of that play.

Oscar and Felix are vivid personalities in the first two acts of *The Odd Couple.* There was no way that Simon could force these two characters to do whatever he wanted them to do in Act Three. The main point dramatized in Act Two is that Oscar and Felix have learned nothing from the failures of their marriages. They are exactly the way they were while married. Because they doggedly insist on asserting their considerable egos, it is abundantly clear they will never change. The "marriage" between them was bound to end in an angry "divorce."

Although Oscar was largely to blame for the failure of his marriage with Blanche, he felt little remorse. That he would instantly be filled with intense guilt feelings about his "breakup" with Felix—a "breakup" for which he was at most only fifty percent to blame—is quite implausible. It is even more unlikely that he, the great bluffer, would almost immediately confess to his friends how guilty he felt. Nor would Felix sincerely assume a major portion of the blame. Rather, he would talk—endlessly, if allowed—about his "flaws," but simultaneously make it clear that all his "flaws" were actually the result of his superiority to Oscar.

Walter Kerr brought the point home when he wrote, "Those two men haven't learned anything from their marital quarrels that will help them share an apartment now, and they aren't going to learn anything from their quarrels now that will help them next time around. . . . They aren't going anywhere, except into new failures."[4] Simon himself perceived this truth, although he did not proceed to honor his perception. In Act Three he presents an insightful exchange between Murray and Oscar. Having just banished Felix, Oscar is already worried about his friend, whom Oscar envisions wandering aimlessly through the streets all night. He tells Murray that the primary reason for his concern is that he was the one who sent Felix out into the night in the first place. Murray contradicts him:

Murray: Frances sent him out in the first place. *You* sent him out in the second place. And whoever he lives with next will send him out in the third place. Don't you understand? It's Felix. He does it to himself.
Oscar: Why?
Murray: I don't know why. *He* doesn't know why. (296)

Simon shows the audience why. Neither Felix nor Oscar will ever live happily with someone else because they are both incapable of doing what Simon in *Barefoot in the Park* wisely suggested people should do. Neither man will compromise. Each is a willful egotist.

Simon, then, has to take "the blame" for creating two main characters who are so vibrantly alive they cannot be mechanically manipulated during the play's closing minutes. Nonetheless, like *Barefoot in the Park*, *The Odd Couple* is, overall, good in so many ways it easily overrides its third-act weaknesses. The play's high quality results not only from its superb delineation of two interesting individuals, but from the incongruous juxtaposition of those two individuals. As Howard Taubman stated, Simon's "instinct for incongruity is faultless."[5] It was, in fact, inevitable that Simon's plays move toward a major emphasis on the incongruous, for Simon sees incongruity as a primary feature of human reality. In his introduction to *The Comedy of Neil Simon,* he describes an argument his wife and he were having in the kitchen. In the middle of the argument, his wife "picked up a frozen veal chop recently left out on the table to defrost, and hurled it at me, striking me just above the right eye. I was so stunned I could barely react; stunned not by the blow nor the intent, but by the absurdity that I, a grown man, had just been hit in the head with a frozen veal chop."[6] So, too, one reason Simon writes comedies instead of tragedies is his acute awareness of how much of a man's life is riddled with comic incongruities.

Oscar and Felix's attempt to share living quarters, it can be argued, is the most captivating dramatization of incongruity Simon has yet created. The two men are wildly incompatible roommates. The humor rises out of their clashing personality traits and domestic habits—and out of how preposterous the very idea of their living together is. They, of course, see nothing incongruous about trying to room together. An awareness of the incongruous depends on a person's ability to remove himself far enough from a situation he is a part of to see that situation from a second, less subjective point of view. Self-love prevents Oscar and Felix from obtaining this perspective. Indeed, the core of *The Odd Couple* is Simon's successful presentation of the serious dangers of self-love.

But perhaps the final triumph of Simon's play is that Oscar Madison and Felix Ungar—and Simon's whole concept of "the odd couple"—have become as much a part of our cultural folklore as Babbitt, Superman, Holden Caulfield, and Archie Bunker.

Chapter Three
Hits and Misses

Sweet Charity

Sweet Charity was inspired by the film *Nights of Cabiria,* directed by Federico Fellini. Bob Fosse saw the movie and within twenty-four hours wrote a nine-page adaptation of the plot, putting the story and characters into an American setting. Then he asked Simon, whom Fosse had worked with on *Little Me,* to develop Fosse's outline into the book for the musical *Sweet Charity.*

In its new version, the plot features a goodhearted dance-hall hostess named Charity who yearns for marriage, a home, and a family. As the play opens, she meets her boyfriend in the park and tells him she has in her pocketbook the money she saved to make a down payment for furniture for their future home. The boyfriend grabs the pocketbook and, in order to insure his escape, pushes Charity into the park lake. Not long afterwards, she chances into the movie star Vittorio Vidal. Vidal dimly recognizes Charity's fine qualities, but is so preoccupied with his present temperamental girl friend he gives Charity short shrift. Still later, Charity meets Oscar Lindquist in a stalled Ninety-second Street "Y" elevator. She helps him avoid panicking, and he, responding to her unselfish nature, invites her out. The two of them fall in love, and Charity thinks her bad luck with men is finally going to end. But Oscar finds out about Charity's line of work, and although he tries to be unconcerned about her sexual history, he ultimately confesses he cannot stop thinking about the men in her past. He jilts her, too. To undercut her sorrow, she reminds herself that this time at least she did not lose her savings. She then marches off to live "hopefully ever after."[1]

The musical had a long Broadway run, yet even many of the critics who liked the show had reservations about it. Nonetheless, the book is nothing Simon need apologize for. The extended sequence centered on Charity and Vidal, a sequence which reaches its comic climax with

Charity hiding in a closet after Vidal's girl friend arrives at his bachelor
quarters, builds quite well. The scene in which Charity and Oscar are
stuck in the elevator is even more amusing. Almost as good is the later
scene when the two lovers are stuck again—this time while on a ride at
Coney Island. There is also a fair sprinkling of funny lines. For example,
when a new girl meets the other dance-hall hostesses, she expresses one
misgiving: she is not a very good dancer. One of the regulars comments,
"Who dances? We defend ourselves to music" (92).

Simon usually manages to make Charity appealing without letting his
material become saccharine. Vidal asks Charity why she took the job at
the dance hall, and she declares it was the "fickle finger of fate." She
guilelessly explains: "People always ask me . . . 'How did you wind up
in that joint?' I got so embarrassed always saying, 'I don't know.' . . . I
guess you're supposed to know *why* you do things or *how* you wind up in
places. . . . Anyway, now when anyone asks me why or how I just say,
'Fickle finger of fate,' and I don't get embarrassed any more" (34). After
Oscar and Charity decide to marry and open a gas station, Oscar begins
to brood about what he considers Charity's sexual promiscuity. When it
appears to Charity that Oscar wants her to tell him about her affairs, she
obligingly says, "I'll tell you everything you want to know." A moment
later, he thinks it would be better if he did not know. She promptly says,
"You won't get one word out of me" (111–12).

Yet, because Charity's personality is so limited, and because her
experiences with men are so repetitiously negative (all the men realize
she is a sweet and generous person, but they all ditch her anyhow),
Simon's character portrait of her wears thin. Unfortunately the book has
nothing else going for it. It is not as frequently clever as Simon's book for
Little Me is. No character in *Sweet Charity* is as entertaining as Otto
Schnitzler or the Prince. Nor is the book satirical or a lighthearted spoof
of anything. As was true with *Little Me*, the book for *Sweet Charity* seems
intended mainly to create a showcase role for its star, and it succeeds in
doing so.

The Star-Spangled Girl

The Star-Spangled Girl was the first theater effort by Simon that was only
moderately successful. While still working on the early scenes in the play,
Simon began to have misgivings about the story. As he had done when he
doubted the quality of *Barefoot in the Park,* he took his unfinished script to
Saint Subber. Once again, Subber reassured Simon his project was worth-

while. Reminding himself how happy the final outcome had been concerning *Barefoot in the Park,* Simon resumed work on *The Star-Spangled Girl.* In this case, though, Simon's instincts were right. The main characters are financially insolvent Andy Hobart and Norman Cornell. In order to avoid eviction from their apartment, where they write their politically radical magazine *Fallout,* Andy responds with fake enthusiasm to the ardor of his landlady while Norman writes copy. When Sophie Rauschmeyer, an Olympic swimmer, moves into the same building, Norman is instantly attracted to her despite her ultraconservative views. Abandoning work on the magazine, he woos Sophie; but his efforts only anger her, especially when he inadvertently causes her to lose her job.

In need of money, Sophie agrees to Andy's suggestion that she work for *Fallout,* a suggestion bred by Andy's desire to get Norman back to work on the next issue. This arrangement backfires. Norman continues to make advances to Sophie, who both spurns him and becomes as attracted to Andy as Norman is to her. Norman happens to discover the other two kissing and threatens to leave. Because Andy is slow to respond with equal intensity to Sophie's affection for him, she, too, threatens to leave. Norman finally calms down enough to resume work on *Fallout.* As his interest in Sophie decreases, Andy's increases. Sophie also decides to stay put, prompted by her belief in free speech and by Andy's growing fondness for her.

The play is woefully weak. Simon himself has pinpointed one basic problem. Discussing the characters' motivations, Simon remarked, "I think it was false in that I chose to say that their physical attraction for one another would win out over their intellectual dislike. In real life, I think, they might have had a brief physical relationship, but their intellectual differences would have been dominant."[2] The play's lack of verisimilitude is apparent in other ways, too. With rare exceptions, the characters in everything Simon previously wrote had no serious political or religious commitments. Andy's prime motivation throughout the play, on the other hand, is his fierce political commitment. Yet the audience never witnesses Andy's political beliefs entering his daily life. Nor is the audience ever told precisely what political targets Andy and Norman are aiming at. (One suspects, of course, that Simon did this in order not to risk alienating members of the audience from his two protagonists.) As a result, the foundation of the plot is impossibly vague.

Other details are also handled in weak or slipshod fashion. One crisis in the play occurs when Andy and Norman, although broke, must pay

their printer's bill for six hundred dollars within a week's time. Yet
approximately nine days elapse before the day arrives for the showdown
with the printer. Their lack of money reduces Norman to eating one
sardine on a frozen waffle for a meal. Nonetheless, he soon starts buying
all kinds of presents for Sophie, including twenty-two dollars' worth of
delicacies from a gourmet shop. That Sophie is supposed to be a swimmer of Olympic caliber is equally unconvincing. A finalist in the
previous Olympic contest, she intends to compete in the next Olympics.
Yet she has no financial arrangement which allows her plenty of practice
time. Nor does she swim according to any training schedule; nor does she
have a coach or trainer.

Because of its flimsy plot and lack of character development, Simon
crammed his play with gags. Some work well. Early in the play, Norman
reports, "I've been pounding the typewriter for nine straight hours. I am
now capable of committing the perfect crime because I no longer have
fingerprints."[3] While wooing Sophie, Norman asks Andy what he could
do for her "that's very small and very personal." Andy suggests, "How
about brushing her teeth?" (315).

Unfortunately, the need to come up with jokes independent of the
flimsy situations in the play led Simon to fall back on his predilection for
the "circular joke." There is this belabored exchange, for instance:

Andy: Why don't you call up a girl?
Norman: You can't just call up a girl. You have to know her first.
Andy: Well, call up a girl you know.
Norman: I don't like any of the girls I know. I only like the girls *you* know.
Andy: All right, call up one of my girls.
Norman: I can't. I don't know them.

An equally lame variation of this kind of joke occurs later in the play.
Andy tells Sophie to "stop following me around the room." When
Sophie says, "Ah'm not followin' you. You're runnin' from *me*!" Andy
replies, "I'm running because you're following" (370–71). This second-
act dialogue is part of a long exchange between Andy and Sophie which
seems to take place primarily just to fill up the time. The same holds true
in Act Three; Andy's attempts to prevent Norman from leaving go on
and on at tedious length.

The climax of the play is dismally contrived. Sophie storms out of the
apartment, but plants herself outside the door, hoping Andy will express
his desire for her return. After Andy finally stops trying to keep Norman

in the apartment, Norman leaves, too—only to return moments later. He never explains why he returns or why he suddenly does not care a fig for Sophie any more. He also makes no mention of the striking fact that Sophie is still standing outside the door. When Sophie reappears, her explanation for returning to work for a magazine she detests is: "Ah may not agree with what you say, but if you stop sayin' it, then no one will disagree and that is not the idea of democracy" (390). Given her personality, this reasoning is completely unconvincing.

No one has been as harsh a critic of this play as Simon himself. Simon has referred to the piece as "the least successful play I've written."[4] Still later, he expressed his feelings even more bluntly: "I wish I could bury *The Star-Spangled Girl*."[5]

First Film Work

Simon did not work on the film versions of either *The Star-Spangled Girl* or his first play, *Come Blow Your Horn,* nor was he connected with the film adaptation of *Sweet Charity.* Still, he did become interested in devising movie scripts. His first venture was to coauthor, with Cesare Zavattini, the screenplay *After the Fox,* based on a story Simon had written.

The plot spotlights Aldo Vanucci, played by Peter Sellers, an often-convicted criminal, who escapes from jail after he hears a rumor stating that his sister Gina has become a prostitute. Vanucci sees Gina propositioning a man on a street in Rome and attacks the man—only to discover that his sister is making a movie. He decides to pretend to make a film himself in order to steal some gold bullion. Posing as a director, he talks Tony Powell, an aging American film actor, into starring in "the film." Powell's manager, however, tips off the police, and Vanucci ends up in jail again.

Brendan Gill labeled *After the Fox* a "mishmash."[6] Bosley Crowther was even more unkind. He wrote, "You would hardly think 'amateurish' (meaning sloppy) would be the word for a film starring Peter Sellers at the head of a pretty good cast and directed by Vittorio de Sica, working from a Neil Simon script. But that's exactly the word for the clutter of nonsense called 'After the Fox.' "[7]

Talking about the film not long after it was released in America, Simon remarked that Peter Sellers and he wanted to make a free-wheeling movie, but Vittorio de Sica pressed for a realistic point of view.

"De Sica didn't speak English," said Simon. "His writer, Cesare Zavattini, didn't speak English. We had an interpreter and Zavattini and I had an argument. Then I realized that Zavattini and I were in accord, but the interpreter didn't agree with either of us."[8] Simon's comment sounds like an attempt to be good humored about a project that undoubtedly caused him much aggravation. The joke's content hints that there must have been many disagreements during the making of the film and many occasions when Simon's wishes were overruled. Therefore, it is pointless to attempt to evaluate Simon's contribution to the film.

The movie version of *Barefoot in the Park* represented the first screenplay Simon wrote based on one of his own plays. Not long afterwards, he scripted *The Odd Couple*. In both cases, Simon strove to transfer his plays to the screen with as little alteration in plot and characterization as possible. Except for some obvious photographic "opening up" of the stories, the movies' material usually duplicated what had been presented on stage. Both movies, especially *The Odd Couple*, were praised by the critics and were successful at the box office.

Nonetheless, gradually Simon chastised himself for not taking the time to study the craft of film scripting as thoroughly as he had that of playwriting.[9] His motivation for his movie work was often too negative—consisting mainly of a desire to protect his original material as much as possible. In retrospect, he did not consider the quality of his first film-scripts as all that high.

Promises, Promises

Simon once remarked that there is "no gratification for a playwright in doing a musical book; all the emotional peaks are sung, not spoken, so you mostly write lead-ins for songs."[10] Thus, although the first musical he wrote the book for, *Little Me,* was a success, Simon—up to the time of *They're Playing Our Song*—made no great effort to become involved in other musical productions. He had worked on *Sweet Charity* primarily as a favor to Bob Fosse. He joined the creators of *Promises, Promises* only because of his high regard for the talents of composer Burt Bacharach and lyricist Hal David. It was a most felicitous decision, for Simon proceeded to write the best book for a musical he has so far created.

Adapted from *The Apartment,* an original screenplay by film director Billy Wilder and I. A. Diamond that was the source of a successful film, *Promises, Promises* features insurance employee Chuck Baxter. The first sentence of the play, spoken by Chuck, defines his basic situation. Chuck states, "The main problem with working as a hundred-and-twelve-dollar-a-week accountant in a seventy-two-story insurance company with assets of over three billion dollars that employs thirty-one thousand two hundred and fifty-nine people here in the New York office alone . . . is that it makes a person feel so God-awful *puny.*"[11] Chuck's lack of self-confidence causes him to fail to impress Fran Kubelik, the coworker he idolizes, and to be unable to refuse doing personal favors for his company superiors. These men, in order to carry on their extramarital affairs more comfortably, pressure him into letting them use his bachelor apartment. What Chuck does not know is that Jeff Sheldrake, one of the more powerful executives in the company, uses Chuck's apartment while attempting to rekindle his affair with Fran. Trying to assert himself a little, Chuck asks Fran out. Fran, contemplating ending her relationship with Sheldrake, accepts the date, but on that same night is smooth-talked by Sheldrake into resuming their affair. Although Fran rightly considers herself more worldly-wise than Chuck, she is gullible enough to believe she is the first girl Sheldrake has "fallen in love" with since he married and that he wants to get a divorce so he can marry her.

The turning point in the story pivots on Fran's compact. She leaves it in Chuck's apartment during her rendezvous with Sheldrake. Chuck finds it and, not knowing to whom it belongs, gives it to Sheldrake, who returns it to Fran. At the company Christmas party, Fran lends Chuck her compact so he can take a look at himself in the new hat he bought. Recognizing the compact, Chuck is jolted to discover the woman he idolized is Sheldrake's mistress. Fran is also jolted at the party. Sheldrake's secretary, Miss Olson, informs Fran that Sheldrake has had affairs through the years with several female employees, including Miss Olson herself, and has handed all the women the same line about getting a divorce and marrying them.

Chuck, miserable and disillusioned, brings Marge, a barroom pickup, to his apartment, where Fran and Sheldrake have met following the party. Chuck discovers that after Sheldrake left, Fran attempted to commit suicide. All of Chuck's anger at Fran vanishes. He quickly gets rid of Marge and manages to save Fran's life—with the help of Dr. Dreyfuss, an apartment neighbor who (because of all the women he sees coming to Chuck's place) thinks Chuck is quite the ladies' man. Because Miss Olson has informed Sheldrake's wife what has been going on, Sheldrake plans to meet with Fran again in order to tell her that he now really can get free from his wife. When Sheldrake pressures Chuck for the use of Chuck's apartment, however, Chuck not only refuses to cooperate but also quits his job. Although she does listen to Sheldrake, Fran decides Chuck is the better man. Fran and Chuck end up celebrating New Year's Eve—and their budding love for each other—in Chuck's apartment.

Although *Promises, Promises* is a touch slow in building momentum, the pace does quicken, and the plot and characters become completely absorbing. The initial slowness is understandable. Simon had to take great care in introducing his "hero" to the audience. A young man who, in order to gain a promotion, lets his middle-age company superiors commit adultery with duped single working girls is not a young man an audience would find naturally appealing. By immediately stressing Chuck's lack of self-confidence, Simon nurtures the audience's sympathy for Chuck. Also, via one of his many alterations of the original story, Simon in the first scene provides Chuck with a second motivation for working late in the office. Chuck stays at his desk not simply to avoid the rush-hour crowd (the reason stated in the movie), but also to do extra work on his own time. Chuck, then, is not a basically lazy, unscrupulous guy who would rather get ahead at his job by immoral means than by doing an honest day's work. Chuck's industry indicates he deserves a promotion on his own merits, but that he has not been given one because he is so unassuming that his good work is taken for granted.

Simon made another significant change early in the story. The first scene between Chuck and Fran takes place before he capitulates to his company superiors' desire to use his rooms. This scene has an innocent boy-meets-girl aura about it. Chuck's shyness and lack of self-confidence are stressed again. His naiveté is reinforced by means of another plot alteration made by Simon. The audience is given "dialogue" between Chuck and Fran which occurs only in Chuck's moony daydreams about Fran. In sum, by the time the first executive fast-talks Chuck into giving up his apartment for an evening, it is apparent that Chuck's acquiescence to the scheme is more the result of his timidity and desire to be a nice guy than his ambition to rise through the company ranks.

Nonetheless, Chuck does let Sheldrake use the apartment in order to ensure himself of a promotion. He is, however, quickly "punished" for doing so. Sheldrake gives him tickets to a professional basketball game to while away the time while Sheldrake is in the apartment. Chuck immediately asks Fran to go to the game with him. Because she plans to end her affair with Sheldrake, Fran agrees to meet Chuck at the sports-arena entrance. When Sheldrake manipulates Fran into spending the whole evening with him, Chuck is left waiting at the entrance all evening for Fran to show up.

Yet, although all this groundwork is necessary and cleverly crafted, the play at first only ambles forward. There is no conflict—hence no tension or suspense—because Chuck never puts up much of a fight about anything. Then, in Scene Six, presenting the "reunion" between Fran and Sheldrake, the play catches fire. Although not as smart a cookie as she thinks she is, Fran is much sharper than Chuck. While Sheldrake easily rolled over Chuck to get what he wanted, now, confronting Fran, Sheldrake has to work hard to achieve his goal. Much sparring between the two "lovers" takes place, for Fran has already been wooed, seduced, and temporarily abandoned—to say nothing of taken for granted—by Sheldrake. Still smarting from Sheldrake's unpredictable behavior, Fran is suspicious about his motive for a new meeting. The opening exchange is:

Sheldrake: Fran . . . Fran, how've you been?
Fran: Fine, Mr. Sheldrake.
Sheldrake: Mr. Sheldrake? Whatever happened to Jeff?
Fran: Yeah, whatever happened to him? (426)

Fran is still emotionally attached to Sheldrake. Nonetheless, she does not quickly fall into his arms, even while he sentimentally reminisces about their early days together. Sheldrake says, "Fran, you know neither one of us wanted it to go this far. . . . That first night we did nothing but sit here and talk until two in the morning." Fran replies laconically, "Yeah, just a couple of innocent kids" (428).

Fran is no timid soul. The relentlessly aggressive Sheldrake is cold and calculating. Together, they dramatize a more hard-nosed view of reality than Simon had presented in his earlier plays. Mr. Baker in *Come Blow Your Horn* and Oscar in *The Odd Couple* are by no means pantywaists. But gruff Mr. Baker loves his two sons enough to yield to them, to some degree, at the end of the play. Oscar's bearish personality has no sharp edges to it. He can be blunt and thoughtless, but he is also full of quick generosity. Fran has only a small "soft spot" inside her; Sheldrake has none at all.

Fran initially pays very little attention to Chuck. She cannot even remember his name. She begins to appreciate him only after she is emotionally stung by Sheldrake enough times to realize that she is not as "superior" to Chuck as she first thought. (She also perceives that while Sheldrake adroitly outmaneuvers her, she will have no great trouble dealing with Chuck.) A shrewd schemer, Sheldrake senses that in order to woo Fran back into his arms he must offer her marriage. Simon makes another significant alteration in the original script at this point. In the movie, Sheldrake remains a bit vague about whether he will split up with his wife or not. In *Promises, Promises* Sheldrake breaks down Fran's defenses by using the precise term "divorce" and by going on to say, "I called my lawyer this morning. I'm going through with it, Fran." When she reminds him that she never asked him to leave his wife (the only unrealistic touch in Simon's portrait of Fran—for surely she must have let Sheldrake know she did not want to remain his mistress forever), Sheldrake states flatly, "It's my decision" (431). At that moment, Fran reenters Sheldrake's trap.

Although some later sequences contain a fair share of musical-comedy romance and sentiment, the element of toughness in Scene Six permeates the rest of the play. Sheldrake's secretary, Miss Olson, proves this point. When she, more than a little tight at the company party, unloads the truth on Fran, she does so in a more sharp-tongued—and funnier— manner than her counterpart in the movie did. She describes from experience the routine Sheldrake always uses. She lets Fran know that several girls have preceded Fran into Sheldrake's "heart," then adds, "When we get two more girls we're going to charter a boat ride to Bear Mountain" (442). She concludes her estimation of Sheldrake with the cynical statement, "What a salesman. If our affair lasted two more days I would have bought insurance from him" (442).

Simon also returns to the matter of Chuck and Fran getting their comeuppance for their moral missteps. Chuck had never concerned himself about the young women the executives were manipulating in order to satisfy their sexual whims. This thoughtlessness sets up the bitter irony involved in Chuck's willingness to aid Sheldrake. Chuck is made to realize that in order to gain a promotion, he has loaned his apartment to an executive who takes to bed the woman Chuck idolizes. The realization staggers him emotionally. Fran is hit almost as hard when she learns she has been played for a prime sucker. It is during this sequence that Fran, looking into her compact, discovers that the mirror is broken. "I like it that way," she decides, because it "makes me look the way I feel" (446). Soon afterward, Chuck, dismayed and heartsick, says, "I disgust me" (447).

During Chuck's stopover at a bar, Simon builds up another character from the film, the pathetic Marge. The emphasis on people living amid illusions is underscored in Marge. She refuses to admit she is a sexual bar-hustler. In contrast to Marge, Fran perceives that she has wrapped an illusion around her life. In Chuck's apartment, she listens to Sheldrake back off from his commitment to leave his wife. Fran recognizes Sheldrake's comments for what they are—a series of flimsy excuses—and she realizes that she has been duped *twice* by him.

The scenes instigated by Fran's suicide attempt do not obliterate the unsentimental point of view established earlier. Simon's major means of avoiding treacle was to utilize the comic potential in another character, Chuck's neighbor Dr. Dreyfuss, even more than the screenplay did. Dreyfuss's comic misinterpretation of the degree of romantic involvement between Chuck and Fran and his stern initial refusal to become involved in what he construes as a tawdry affair puncture any possibility of the sequence's bogging down in romantic schmaltz. So does Dreyfuss's nervous interest in himself. When Chuck and Dreyfuss start walking Fran back and forth to keep her awake after she has taken sleeping pills, Dreyfuss comments, "Now comes the dangerous part." Chuck, fearful about Fran's chances to survive, immediately asks the doctor what he means. Dreyfuss replies, "We gotta walk her around a couple of hours. I have to be careful I don't get a heart attack" (463).

As Fran and Chuck talk and play cards while she recuperates, Fran's toughness is diluted by her having been humiliated and by her growing affection for "a square" like Chuck. Simultaneously, Chuck becomes tougher and more self-confident. Simon's story implies that people should be tough, although not as cold and hard as Sheldrake. They need to be tough because the world around them is in no small part composed of Sheldrakes who will hurt them if they are defenseless. People must be able to protect what is warm and loving—and vulnerable—inside them. Thus, Fran quite rightly does not strip away all the hard edges in her personality. Nor does Chuck turn away from Fran because she is not the Miss Innocence he originally daydreamed she was. He accepts the fact he was foolish to be so naive. Now he loves and admires the actual person Fran is.

In this play the changes in the main characters' personalities that bring about a happy ending are changes those characters would realistically undergo—not alterations resulting solely from the author's desire to impose a happy ending upon his material. It is plausible that Chuck would rebuff Sheldrake when the latter presses for the use of the apartment still again. It is equally plausible that Fran, offered a legitimate chance to marry Sheldrake, would have gained enough insight into Sheldrake, Chuck, and herself to turn down the proposal and return to Chuck. It is also plausible, and charming, that the lovers do not madly embrace at the climax. When Chuck, while getting out a deck of cards, pauses to tell Fran he adores her, she says, "I heard you. Now shut up and play cards" (493).

Chapter Four
Plaza Suite

Both *The Odd Couple* and *Promises, Promises* indicate that Simon was gravitating toward writing comedies consisting of more than a stream of funny lines. *Plaza Suite,* a highly successful blend of humor and character study, completes the transition. Later, discussing his shift to this goal, Simon stated, "I used to ask, 'What is a funny situation?' Now I ask, 'What is a sad situation and how can I tell it humorously?'"[1]

"Visitor from Mamaroneck"

Plaza Suite consists of three one-act plays, all taking place in the same hotel suite. The first play, "Visitor from Mamaroneck," depicts the marital situation of Karen and Sam Nash. Aware that her husband has become increasingly indifferent to her after more than twenty years of marriage, Karen suspects he is having an affair with his secretary, Jean McCormack. So, while their house is repainted, Karen rents what she believes to be the same suite that Sam and she stayed in on their honeymoon. She has bought a sexy negligee and has deliberately not packed any pajamas for Sam. Sam soon joins her, but is totally preoccupied with his looks and with completing a big business deal. When Miss McCormack appears with data containing an error, Sam decides the two of them must meet back at the office to check the problem out. After Miss McCormack leaves, Karen confronts Sam with the fact that their marriage is deteriorating and asks him if he is having an affair with his secretary. Eventually Sam confesses he is. At first Karen tells him she will accept his need for an affair with a younger woman; later, she asks him to end the affair. Although he loves Karen, Sam will not agree to her request and leaves to meet his secretary.

While *Promises, Promises* dealt with a husband and "the other woman," this one-acter centers on the conflict between the husband and wife. Simon stresses two additional conflicts—the turmoil within the husband

and, above all, the turmoil within the wife. Initially, Karen is trying solely to keep the lid on the situation. Her goal is simply to rekindle the love Sam and she felt for each other in the early years of their marriage. She believes that if she can do that, she can defuse any problems bred by the deterioration of the marriage.

That her plan is a calculated one does not mean she has attained a coolly detached view of her predicament. On the contrary, the tension Karen feels is readily apparent. Learning from the bellhop that a famous New York building has been torn down, she immediately applies this fact to her own situation. She says that is how things are these days: if something is old, it is torn down. Other facets of Karen's personality are quickly revealed. She is a scrapper, which prepares the audience for Karen's later confrontation with Sam. Indeed, she fights even when she is sure she will lose. Before Sam arrives, she orders some hors d'oeuvres over the phone, stressing that she does not want any anchovies. Yet she expects (justifiably, as it turns out) that she will be served anchovies all the same. It is equally plausible that Karen would suspect the truth concerning Sam and his secretary, for she is remarkably willing to confront the truth. The stage directions state, "Karen is forty-eight years old, and she makes no bones about it."[2] She looks in the mirror and declares, "You are definitely some old lady" (500). Karen's honesty, however, has done more than lead her to realize her marriage is in trouble; it is one of the basic reasons the marriage *is* in trouble. Her husband will not accept that he is aging, and he resents Karen's acceptance of middle age. He even encourages her to lie about her age.

With Sam's entrance, the plot focuses directly on the marital relationship. It becomes clear that Sam expects Karen to concentrate selflessly on his needs and desires, but that when she does so, he takes her for granted. He recognizes her individual existence only when she fails to aid him competently. Karen's perceptiveness and her desire for a particularly pleasant evening with her husband pull her in two directions. Her suspicions concerning the possibility of Sam's infidelity mount. For one thing, although Sam explains his gruffness with her by stating he has a bad headache, he is all charm while talking with Miss McCormack on the phone. He also sidesteps Karen's comment that she has seen less and less of him at night in the past month. Still, she resolutely resumes cajoling Sam.

The situation intensifies when Sam decides he must meet Miss McCormack back at the office. Watching Sam primp and shave in front of the mirror, Karen intuits that Sam and Miss McCormack have previously arranged to meet this evening. Crushingly disappointed that her plan for a special evening with her husband is collapsing, she asks him if he is having an affair with his secretary. At first Sam denies everything. Then Karen says that "if at this stage" of Sam's life he wants to have "a small, quiet affair with a young, skinny woman," she would understand. Instantly Sam replies, "What do you mean, at this stage of my life?" (527).

Now the play scrutinizes Sam's character—for Karen has hit Sam where he lives. Earlier, Karen had lamented, "I'm not insane about getting older. It happens to everyone. It's happened to you. You're fifty-one years old." Sam retorted, "That's the difference between us. I don't accept it. I don't have to accept being fifty-one" (521). Karen's newest allusion to his age leads Sam for the first time to open up to Karen—and to himself. He takes primary responsibility for their marriage turning sour. Next, he confesses, "When I came home after the war . . . I had my whole life in front of me. And all I dreamed about, all I wanted, was to get married, and to have children . . . and to make a success of my life. . . . Well, I was very lucky. . . . I got it all. . . . Marriage, the children . . . more money than I ever dreamed of making." Puzzled, Karen asks, "Then what is it you want?" Sam blurts, "I just want to do it all over again . . . I would like to start the whole damned thing right from the beginning."

Karen's response to this poignant disclosure may be interpreted as a gag designed to keep the play from becoming too serious. She says, "Well, frankly, Sam, I don't think the Navy will take you again." It *is* a funny comeback. But it is more than that. Her remark reminds Sam that he cannot go back in time. It asks him to accept his present situation. For Karen senses that if Sam will accept the reality of his situation, their marriage has a chance.

Consequently, when Sam replies in turn, "Well, it won't be because I can't pass the physical," Karen is deeply shaken. She realizes that their marriage is in an even more precarious state than she previously surmised it was. She bluntly, unhumorously says aloud exactly what she is thinking: "I think you want to get out and you don't know how to tell me" (529). When Sam starts to leave, Karen for the first time lashes out at him, demanding that he stay and discuss their situation. Rocked again when Sam confesses that he is having an affair with his secretary, Karen reneges on her willingness to go along with such a development.

Karen is caught in a cruel dilemma. She knows that if she does not battle to break up the affair, Sam, in his obsession to "keep young," will become so enamored of Miss McCormack he will seek a divorce. Yet Karen is equally aware that if she pressures Sam to end the affair, she will become in his eyes a nagging, unattractive woman. She tells him she knows her criticism of him "makes everything nice and simple for you. Now you can leave here the martyred, misunderstood husband" (534). At her wit's end, she pleads with Sam to stay in the suite with her. Sam, however, will not let himself surrender to age. Although his awareness that Karen is a fine woman prevents him from deciding then and there to divorce her, he feels he has to leave—at least for this night.

Neither of them knows if he will come back.

"Visitor from Hollywood"

In the second sketch, "Visitor from Hollywood," movie producer Jesse Kiplinger arranges a meeting in his suite with his old high-school girlfriend Muriel Tate. Muriel, well aware that Jesse has become famous, is both intrigued and intimidated by his fame. She talks about leaving for home throughout the early stages of the conversation. After Jesse tells her that his private life is as much of a failure as his professional life is a success, Muriel relaxes. They begin kissing. Later, while Jesse starts to remove her dress, Muriel starts asking him gossipy questions about other famous Hollywood personalities.

As in the previous one-acter, Simon uses a familiar situation. The first story features the eternal triangle. The situation in this second one-acter is that of the cosmopolitan male's attempt to seduce the uncosmopolitan female. Simon breathes new life into this situation by focusing not on the act of seduction, but on the motivations of the seducer and the seduced. Simon shows how complicated a simple seduction can be. The seduction is simple because both Jesse and Muriel want it to take place. What complicates matters is that each wants more out of the seduction than a sexual interlude.

Initially, Muriel is so impressed by Jesse's fame she is uncertain she can be a satisfactory sexual partner. After they kiss, she nervously asks Jesse, "Was it good?" Startled, he only after a moment or two has the presence of mind to reply, "It was a superb kiss" (547). Another problem arises when, early in the conversation, Jesse brushes aside Muriel's questions about glamorous Hollywood because he does not want to be reminded of his life out there. He wants to recapture the manly confidence he felt when young. Disillusioned by his personal experiences while in California, he sees Muriel as a symbol of his comparatively more innocent pre-Hollywood life. After their high-school years, however, Muriel's life became dismally mundane; and she is not at all interested in reliving "days gone by." Jesse's appeal for her is precisely that he symbolizes the Hollywood life-style she fantasizes about. When, for instance, he blurts out that his newest picture is "a piece of crap" (546), Muriel will have none of it. She quotes how much money it has made and ponders its chances of winning an Academy Award.

As a result, for a good while, no seduction takes place. Instead, each of them continues to pursue his or her private obsession. Jesse elaborates on his renewed interest in Muriel by telling her she is "the only, solitary, real, honest-to-goodness, unphoney woman" (548) he has been with since he went to Hollywood seventeen years ago. He tells her he remembers exactly what she wore the day he left her to go to Hollywood. He begs her never to change from "the sweet, simple way you are" (550). Muriel does not follow Jesse's lead. When he speaks of the day he left for California, Muriel states, "I remember when your first picture came to Tenafly" (549). All her reflections concerning their high-school years and her life thereafter relate directly to his later success. She informs him that their old high-school friends tease her, telling her, "If I married you instead of Larry, I'd be living in Hollywood now" (549). In response to his pleas that she never change, she says, "Do you know Frank Sinatra?" (550). More than a little drunk on vodka stingers, Muriel blurts out, "I suppose you'll go back to Hollywood and have a big laugh with Otto Preminger over this" (551).

Jesse's preoccupation with himself finally subsides enough for him to become aware of Muriel's fear of inadequacy. Quickly he begins reassuring her that he has only the warmest feelings for her. Then, as a further means of wooing Muriel, but also because he sincerely needs to express the unhappiness churning within him, Jesse tells Muriel the truth about himself. He confesses he has been humiliated both financially and sexually by his three former wives. Staggered by these defeats, he yearns for the unthreatening atmosphere of innocence he is convinced existed back when he dated Muriel. He wants this so much he ignores a blatantly obvious fact—namely, that Muriel is not now (if she ever was) the uncomplicated high-school sweetheart he persists in believing she still is. He also does not confront the pathetic contradiction in, on the one hand, his delight in Muriel's supposed innocence and, on the other hand, his desire to have sexual intercourse with her in order to reassure himself about his sexual prowess.

Jesse's confession provides the pivotal turn in his present relationship with Muriel. His words stoke Muriel's self-confidence. Previously, she had shuttled back and forth concerning how much free time she had. Now she relaxes and declares, "I've got plenty of time" (554). She completes the job of getting drunk. She admits her own marriage is a mess. She literally not once, but twice throws her arms around Jesse. And she insists he tell her some Hollywood gossip.

Sensing "victory," Jesse states what truly does express the sad— vain—hope both Muriel and he have. He says, "The world can change for one hour" (558).

Thus, both Muriel's daydream and Jesse's "come true." She is made love to by a Hollywood Celebrity. He makes love to an Innocent Woman. Muriel does not want to see, beneath the celebrity, a pathetically insecure, egotistical human being interested only in reasserting his masculinity by sleeping with a middle-aged groupie. Jesse ignores the fact Muriel has become a frustrated, calculating, hard-drinking housewife. On this day both Jesse and Muriel fornicate a fantasy. Consequently, they do not change their drab lives one iota.

Thematically, this one-acter ties in with the other two segments of *Plaza Suite* and with other writings by Simon. As Edythe M. McGovern observed concerning Jesse, Sam Nash, and Roy Hubley, the main male character in the third one-acter, "There is an interesting commonality among the three principal male characters. . . . Each man has achieved the visible trappings of success as our middle-class world views that phenomenon. Each has reached the forty to fifty age bracket and somehow discovered that 'winning the goal' does not necessarily bring the satisfactions associated with that feat."[3] Jesse and Muriel also prove a point Simon dramatizes through the characters in *Last of the Red-Hot Lovers*, through Faye Medwick and Leo Schneider in *Chapter Two*, and through the Fran Kubelik/Jeff Sheldrake relationship in *Promises, Promises*—namely, that a relationship founded on sex without love is an emotionally bankrupt relationship.

"Visitor from Forest Hills"

The third one-act play is much lighter fare. In "Visitor from Forest Hills" a prospective bride, Mimsey, locks herself in the suite's bathroom minutes before she is to be married. Unable to entice Mimsey out of the bathroom, Norma, her mother, phones her husband, Roy, downstairs.

As soon as he arrives on the scene, he, too, attempts to convince Mimsey to unlock the bathroom door. He also attempts to break the door down and to climb in through the bathroom window. Finally, when her parents converse with her more calmly, Mimsey tells them what is bothering her. Still, she does not come out of the bathroom until her fiancé comes to speak to her.

Here Simon presents in semifarcical fashion the problems of communication and of making a serious commitment to another person when one is intensely aware of the dangers involved. The first problem dominates. When Norma phones downstairs, her future son-in-law's father is the first one to speak with her, and she tells him everything is going along beautifully; the instant her husband gets on the phone her suppressed desperation explodes in words. Yet it is only when Roy enters the suite that she tells him exactly what the problem is. For a minute, Roy does not believe what Norma tells him; then he pigheadedly decides that Norma must have caused the problem by saying the wrong thing to Mimsey.

The problem of communicating is even more effectively dramatized when, before Roy arrives, Norma tells Mimsey, "I know what you're going through now, sweetheart, you're just nervous." Failing to gain an immediate response from Mimsey, Norma shouts, "Mimsey, if you don't care about your life, think about mine. Your father'll kill me" (561). What becomes increasingly clear is that, in large part, Mimsey refuses to come out of the bathroom because her parents fail to use the right approach with her. Norma should have continued concentrating on what Mimsey was thinking and feeling on her wedding day. Instead, Norma selfishly switched her concern to herself—to her fear about what Roy would say to her when he discovered what Mimsey had done.

Norma's selfishness is more than matched by her husband's. As soon as he enters the suite he says, "Why are you standing here? There are sixty-eight people down there drinking my liquor" (562). Roy's first words to Mimsey are, "This is your father. I want·you and your four-hundred-dollar wedding dress out of there in five seconds!" (564). He asks Mimsey nothing; nor does he offer to discuss the situation. He simply issues a command stressing what preoccupies him most—the amount of money that the wedding is costing him.

Both Norma and Roy proceed to pay dearly for their almost continuous self-absorption. Norma rips her stockings while trying to peek through the bathroom-door keyhole. Later, pounding on the door, she breaks her diamond ring. Roy almost breaks his arm when he rams his shoulder into the door. His coat is ripped as he attempts to climb into the bathroom via the window.

Only when Norma begins to concentrate on how Mimsey feels do the parents make any progress. At one point, she exclaims to Roy, "Is that all you care about? What it's costing you? Aren't you concerned about your daughter's happiness?" (565). Later, in a moment of exhaustion, Norma says to Roy, "I'll tell you who can get into that bathroom. Someone with love and understanding. Someone who cares about that poor kid who's going through some terrible decision now and needs help. Help that only *you* can give her and that *I* can give her" (577). Momentarily humbled by this insight, Roy for the first time tries seriously to communicate with his daughter. Soon Mimsey talks quietly with him in the bathroom, after which Roy phones the bridegroom, Borden, and asks him to come up. Roy then explains to Norma that their daughter is afraid that Borden and she will become exactly like her parents, whose marriage, filled with incessant bickering, the audience has just seen on display.

When Borden arrives, Roy says, "It seems you're the only one who can communicate with her." Borden strides to the bathroom door and says, "Mimsey? . . . This is Borden. . . . Cool it!" (581). With these few comically cryptic words—and the strength and reassurance offered in his tone and manner—Borden has communicated with Mimsey. Mimsey comes out of the bathroom. Her parents, who have exchanged thousands of words with each other, but who have rarely communicated love for one another, are left bewildered. So, they once again do what they have always done: they turn on each other. Roy says, "What kind of a person is that to let your daughter marry?" Norma snaps back, "Roy, don't aggravate me. I'm warning you" (582).

Despite the faint scent of sadness that permeates the atmosphere of all three segments of *Plaza Suite,* especially the first two, many critics regarded Simon's latest comedy as no different from all his previous work. Or they considered it retrogressive. Walter Kerr was more perceptive. He wrote that "a shadow of substance has become the base for the joke" in Simon's comedies. Kerr went on to point out that Americans tend to disbelieve that a comedy can contain any serious point. He stated, "One of the crazy mistakes we make in the contemporary theater is that in supposing that if something is serious at all it must be thoroughly, thumpingly serious." Kerr concluded: "There *are* small truths . . . truths of a size that can be accommodated in—and almost cheerfully covered over by—a quip."[4] Amid the laughter it evokes,

Plaza Suite offers incisive character delineations that dramatize several insights into human experience. To perceive these insights, however, and to perceive the high quality of Simon's finest creative achievements, one must accept the possibility that a writer can simultaneously make people laugh and offer them valuable insights.

Chapter Five
Last of the Red-Hot Lovers

Although *Last of the Red-Hot Lovers,* like *Plaza Suite,* is a mixture of character delineation, humor, and observations about contemporary life, there are important differences in the two plays. While all three segments of *Plaza Suite* are soundly constructed, the second act of *Last of the Red-Hot Lovers* is flawed. On the other hand, in the later play Simon scrutinizes various attitudes toward the human experience more intently and directly than he ever ventured to do before.

Plaza Suite featured three couples occupying the same rooms over a period of approximately six months. *Last of the Red-Hot Lovers* spotlights one man, Barney Cashman, and the three women he directs, in turn, to his mother's apartment during the course of ten months' time. The first woman to join Barney in the apartment is Elaine Navazio, who frequented the restaurant he owns. Barney, aware of the sexual revolution going on throughout the country, wants one romantic extramarital experience before he moves toward old age. Elaine simply wants sex. In his attempt to make the encounter more than a merely sexual one, Barney keeps talking and talking until Elaine becomes irritated and walks out.

Although Barney vows never again to try to set up an extramarital sexual tryst, he forsakes his vow nine months later. Accidentally meeting Bobbi Michele in the park one afternoon, he lends her money so she can hire an accompanist for her theater audition. The next day, she comes to his mother's apartment, supposedly in order to pay him back. She sees, though, that Barney will not pressure her either for the money or for sexual favors in lieu of the money. She also perceives that her descriptions of her "far out" life fascinate him; so she makes herself comfortable, talks at great length, and finally badgers Barney into smoking some marijuana with her before she leaves.

Within a month, Barney arranges a rendezvous with Jeanette Fisher. Jeanette and her husband, Mel, are good friends of Barney and his wife,

Thelma. Barney is much more aggressive than he was on the two previous occasions. Jeanette, however, brooding about Mel's having an affair with another woman, is too depressed to follow through on her previous impulse to have sex with Barney. Instead, she leads Barney into a debate about whether there are any decent people in the world. Barney ultimately convinces her there are. Feeling less melancholy, Jeanette leaves. Barney phones his wife, Thelma, and tries to coax her into coming to the apartment for sex.

Barney, like the three husbands in *Plaza Suite,* is undergoing a middle-age crisis. Barney's crisis, however, is not caused by a desire to be young again, or by the need to prove his sexual prowess and rebuild his self-confidence, or by a daughter who bewilders him. Barney has become intensely aware of his own mortality. Realizing that he has settled into a bland life-style, and that other people's lives are freer and more exciting, Barney wants more out of his life.

When Elaine Navazio responds to his overtures while in his restaurant, Barney gives her the address of his mother's apartment and hurries there to wait for her. The setting symbolizes part of Barney's inner conflict. The building is new, but the furniture is old, "from another generation."[1] Barney and his values are from another, more conservative generation; but now, like the younger generation, he wants to "swing"—at least a little. His conflicting desires are underscored very quickly in the opening scene. Barney tells Elaine that she looks like someone who should be named Irene. She looks in the mirror and remarks, "No, I look like an Elaine Navazio" (587). Barney wants to see Elaine as an "Irene"—see her within a romantic context. Elaine sticks to reality. Thus, long before Barney articulates the point aloud, it is evident that he wants sex, but that he wants it to be part of a romantic interlude. Elaine wants a brief, intense sexual coupling.

Elaine relishes living on a sensuous level. She wants cigarettes, which she forgot to bring, and many refills of her liquor glass. She speaks straightforwardly and specifically of Barney's physically attractive features. She tells Barney that she gets intense cravings to "eat, to touch, to smell, to see, to do," and that for her a "sensual, physical pleasure" can only "be satisfied at *that* particular moment" (594–95). By no coincidence, then, she is the one who keeps bringing the conversation back to the question of when are they going to have sex.

Barney is shocked and dismayed by her directness and her starkly limited desires. While insisting he is not a prude, he repeatedly stresses that he does not want "just" a sexual encounter. He describes his intentions as "of a romantic nature" (598). In defense of choosing his mother's unexotic apartment for their meeting, he says, "I thought a motel was a little sordid" (599). When Elaine complains about Barney's incessant talking, he explains, "I just thought you might be interested in knowing a little bit more about me" (599). Goaded by her jibes, he says, "I find it disturbing, and a little sad, that your attitude towards people is so detached" (601). In sum, he cannot, after all, be like the young swingers he has heard about who have sex, plain and straight, with total strangers.

Nervous and upset, he ultimately succeeds in "humanizing" his encounter with Elaine even more than he wanted to. As Jesse Kiplinger did with Muriel Tate, Barney reveals more about himself and his problems than he originally intended to do. He tells Elaine that other than with his wife, he has had only one sexual experience in his whole life: one night when he was young his brother took him to a middle-aged whore in New Jersey. He goes on to say that although he is for all practical purposes a success in life, he feels he has missed out on many things. What aroused this feeling in him was his increasing awareness of death—that "for the first time in my life I think about dying" (611). He became unhappy that he could be aptly described in one word: "nice." He asked himself, "Shouldn't there be something else besides opening the restaurant eleven o'clock every morning?" (611). So, he started daydreaming about having one extramarital experience, "an experience so rewarding and fulfilling that it would last me the rest of my life" (612).

Seeking to make his daydream come true, Barney gets far more than he bargained for, just as Chuck did when he pursued his dream girl, Fran, in *Promises, Promises*. For one thing, Elaine tells him, "If you want undying love and romance, take a guitar and go to Spain" (608). She also informs him that the whore he slept with might well have been her mother. When he preaches to her and inquires about her marriage, she lashes out, "I didn't come up here to get reformed," and tells him to "leave my sex life alone" (600).

Elaine does not want to analyze her situation, for she does not have any hope of improving her lot in life. She simply wants a moment of unthinking sensuous pleasure. She states, "I happen to like the pure physical act of making love. It warms me, it stimulates me and it makes me feel like a woman" (609). In other words, while Jesse Kiplinger and

Muriel Tate kid themselves into believing that "the world can change for one hour," Elaine entertains no such illusion. She believes nothing will change the basically bleak human condition. By the time the third-act curtain falls, the play reveals that in Simon's opinion Elaine's outlook is excessively grim. Thus, when, at his most sentimental, Barney describes Elaine as "sad and pitiful" (608), his description is not without validity. Yet Elaine, stung by this description, touches on the truth, too. She retorts that Barney is the pitiful one—and so much of a hypocrite that he should be in no hurry to pass judgment on others. She points out to him that as much as he is presently concerned about "poor" Elaine, once their afternoon together ends he will pray fervently that she never enters his restaurant again. She declares, "I don't know your problems and I don't care. . . . No one really cares about anything or anyone in this world except himself." She concludes that the only sensible guideline is: "If you can't taste it, touch it or smell it, forget it!" (609).

Timidly exploring the world at large, Barney has met someone living in a state of resigned, yet intense desperation that minimizes—at least temporarily—his middle-aged awareness that he will eventually die. In fact, Elaine is in far worse physical shape than Barney is. She repeatedly is racked by coughing fits so severe she is forced to hold onto furniture in order to keep from collapsing. Near the end of their rendezvous, Elaine tells Barney that "no one gives a good crap about you dying because a lot of people discovered it ahead of you. We're all dying, Mr. Cashman" (612).

Elaine's attack on Barney's musings about the human condition articulates a view of reality unmatched in fierceness by any other character's philosophy of life in any Simon play to date. It is a far tougher point of view, for instance, than either Fran's or Sheldrake's in *Promises, Promises*. It is so powerful that Barney will only begin to try fumblingly to undercut Elaine's beliefs ten months later—in Act Three—when he arranges to meet Jeanette in the apartment. A major flaw in Act Two is that it barely touches on the challenge Elaine's philosophy of life presented to Barney.

Nine months after his talk with Elaine, Barney again ventures beyond the world he knows best. Having helped Bobbi Michele out financially, he hopes his rendezvous with her will culminate in sex. But Bobbi comes at Barney from too many directions for him to steer her where he wants to go. It is not really even a matter of Bobbi defeating him in a battle of wills, for no conflict takes place. Barney almost immediately bogs down in merely trying to figure Bobbi out. Eventually, he gives up the effort. He is reduced to being a fascinated listener whom she pressures into operating on her terms. What dilutes dramatic interest still further is that, like Barney, the audience has no way of figuring Bobbi out. Various interpretations of Bobbi's character are suggested via her chatter early on. Unfortunately the rest of the scene merely keeps circling back to those same possible interpretations. It is no wonder that during the tryout period Simon worked more on this middle act than on the other two.

One of the few things that can be said about Bobbi with confidence is that she does not have a firm grip on reality. Not long after she arrives at the apartment, she says, "I love this neighborhood. . . . I once had a girl friend who lived on this block. Forty-seventh between First and York." Barney has to correct her: "This is Thirty-seventh" (615). She also tells Barney he is shorter than he looked the day before, and that she remembered him as having a moustache.

At times she appears to be one of life's helpless victims. Barney, for instance, feels sorry for Bobbi while she tells him a man in the airplane seat next to hers pawed her during a recent flight. Barney is startled to learn soon afterward that she gave her "assailant" her phone number. She complains about receiving obscene phone calls; but then it turns out that, instead of hanging up, she listens to the obscenities for fifteen minutes at a clip. She is sometimes equally misleading when describing less bizarre episodes in her life. Speaking about her audition the day before, she tells Barney that David Merrick thought she was fabulous. Pressed by Barney about this reference to Merrick, she backs off, claiming only that *someone* with a moustache sitting out front praised her. She adds that she would have gotten the part, but the producers wanted a black girl. Yet when Barney later mentions she was turned down at the audition, she snaps, "I didn't say they turned me down. I said they took the black girl" (631).

Bobbi's angry outburst points to another facet of her personality. She undergoes sudden shifts of mood. When a roommate is slow to answer Bobbi's phonecall, Bobbi stops her blithe chatter and remarks coldly, "She hears the phone. She's just a lazy bitch" (620). Nor is she always as naive as she would like Barney to believe. More than a little paranoiac, she laments how cruel people have been to her, including the men with whom she has supposedly had affairs. Then she shrewdly comments, "Married men are rarely vicious. They're too guilty" (624). Although she appears not to listen to what Barney says, he mumbles something about smoking marijuana with her sometime, and later she reminds him of his promise and forces him to light up.

The only mild suspense in this scene resides in the question: what will Bobbi say next? But the audience's curiosity concerning the degree of truth in Bobbi's stories is stymied by there being no objective means of comparing her statements with the reality of her situation. All one can safely say is that while such characters as the "lovers" Jesse and Muriel tried to live an illusion, Bobbi's problem is much worse. She has no more than a tenuous hold on reality.

Still, some of the dialogue near the end of Act Two is important thematically to the play as a whole. Bobbi reassures Barney—and herself—that it is only a matter of time before others recognize her genuine talent as a performer. Then, in another shift of mood, she paranoiacally insists, "People don't want to see you make good . . . they're all jealous . . . they're all rotten . . . they're all vicious" (635). This declaration, as Edythe M. McGovern has pointed out, somewhat parallels Elaine Navazio's outlook on life.[2] Thus, Bobbi's statement reminds the audience that the challenge to refute this outlook has still not been met.

Bitter because she was turned down at the audition, Bobbi speaks of gaining revenge on the world by writing a book telling of all her encounters with men. Barney is instantly nervous. He says, "I'm sure once in a while you must have met some *nice* men" (629). She calms him down by reassuring him that she will not mention someone as sensitive as him in her book. Significantly, Barney no longer sees his being a "nice" person in a totally negative light.

In Act Two, while high on marijuana, Barney muses, "So many things I wanted to do . . . but I'll never do 'em," and adds, "Trapped . . . we're all trapped" (635). Yet, less than a month later, he makes one last attempt to wriggle out of the "trap" he is in and find an extramarital sexual moment of bliss. Responding to remarks his friend Jeanette makes at a social gathering, Barney arranges a rendezvous with her. Like Elaine and Bobbi, Jeanette has a grim view of life. Jeanette, however, is markedly different from the other two women. She does not try to suppress or evade her darker moods. On the contrary, she wallows in depression. While Elaine escapes into sensual pleasure and Bobbi into fantasy and paranoia, Jeanette broods about the human condition.

Typically, Simon wastes little time setting things into motion. Moments after she enters the apartment, Jeanette begins to sob. As soon as she stops sobbing, she says, "Why am I here, Barney?" (637). The range of Jeanette's probing will not prove very wide. She will make no serious references to religious creeds, politics, or philosophical tenets. Nonetheless, she will, in her tense, fretful way, ask fundamental questions. Employing a realistic and comic framework, Simon shows Jeanette and Barney stumbling toward these questions. Jeanette does say early on that she thinks Barney is "basically a good person" (638)—an important point they will return to; but the comment is made amid a series of remarks that deflate Barney, for Jeanette is busy stressing how physically unattractive she finds Barney. Barney at this time is totally uninterested in fundamental questions. The defeats he suffered in his previous extramarital encounters have honed his sexual frustrations to a keen edge. He is now in almost the exact frame of mind that Elaine was in ten months earlier. He does not want chitchat. He wants sex.

Ironically, Barney has waited too long and has picked the wrong partner for his current mood. Jeanette is as unsensuous a person as Elaine was sensuous. Elaine craved certain foods; Jeanette states, "I can *not* taste food" (643). Jeanette also tells Barney, "I don't particularly enjoy sex" (639). Embodying a somber moral awareness and a strong sense of guilt, she is appalled by the same contemporary promiscuity that so intrigues Barney. Barney tries to ply Jeanette with drinks, but she doggedly states, "You're not going to have a good time with me" (642).

Barney wanted to humanize his relationship with Elaine by finding out something about her. With Jeanette, Barney keeps trying to dodge her attempts to instigate a meaningful conversation. Jeanette asks him if her husband, Mel, has talked to Barney about her. Barney brushes aside the very possibility. He does the same thing when Jeanette inquires whether Mel ever spoke to him about Mel's affair with another woman. She asks him if he feels guilty about meeting her in the apartment. Exasperated, Barney finally says to Jeanette, "Why probe deeply into everything?" (641).

Barney's success at avoiding Jeanette's attempts to draw him into a serious conversation ends when Jeanette asks him if he thinks death is terrible. This question snags him. For it was his intensified awareness of death that nurtured his desire for an affair. He replies that he does think death is terrible. Jeanette immediately follows up with another question, "You mean you enjoy your life?" Barney, all seriousness now, responds, "I *love* living. I have some problems with my *life,* but living is the best thing they've come up with so far" (644).

Because Jeanette sincerely wants to learn some affirmative reasons why she should go on living, she asks Barney how much of life he actually enjoys. Pressed for a precise answer, he says, "Fifty-one, fifty-two

percent" (645). Jeanette then asks him if he thinks there are many decent
people in the world, and Barney resumes trying to sidestep Jeanette's
series of questions. When she challenges him to name three decent
people, however, he—hoping to wrap the whole matter up and get on
with the sex—allows himself to accept the challenge. Barney cites his
wife, Thelma, as one of the three.

Jeanette is reluctant to put Thelma on her list of three immediately,
and now, thoroughly exasperated, Barney begins to shuttle back and
forth in mood. He, on the one hand, again wants to blot out the whole
conversation by focusing strictly on sex. He becomes increasingly sexually aggressive—almost threatening. On the other hand, he is gnawed at
by the still unresolved question of what should be the final judgment of
human beings. At one point, he claims, "We're not indecent, we're not
unloving. We're human" (650). Later, sexually impatient, he tells
Jeanette, "All right, we're all no good" (652).

The climax of the play, the climax that Simon has been moving
toward—albeit not all that steadily—since Act One occurs when
Jeanette, genuinely frightened by Barney's sexual advances, begs him to
stop. She blurts out, "I know you're not like this," and goes on to say,
"You're quiet. You're intelligent." Then she exclaims, "You're decent!
You *are*, Barney!" (654–55). These statements stop Barney in his tracks.
In Act One, a comment by Elaine made Barney realize he unconsciously
and fruitlessly kept trying to rid his hands of the smell of the fish he
prepared for the customers in his restaurant. Jeanette's comments make
him equally aware that—as he said to Bobbi—"We're all trapped." Just
as he can never rid his hands of the smell of fish, he can never escape from
the trap of his basic nature. Barney gains the same humbling but helpful
self-knowledge that all four characters in *Barefoot in the Park* and Fran in
Promises, Promises gained—and that Oscar and Felix in *The Odd Couple*
never gained. Barney finally accepts that he will never be a part of the
new sexual revolution, for he is precisely the type of man he told Elaine
he was—a nice guy.

Abandoning his sexual scheme, Barney gets Jeanette to admit that
Thelma is gentle, loving, and decent. He makes Jeanette see that,
however many other kinds of people there are in the world, a significant
number of people are decent, even though these people—because they
are human—are imperfect. Paradoxically, thanks to Barney and to her
own insistence on confronting her problems, although Jeanette originally wallowed in melancholy, she leaves the apartment much less
imprisoned by depression than Elaine and Bobbi.

Despite all the plays and movie scripts he wrote after *Last of the Red-Hot Lovers,* Simon thus far in his career has never come any closer to stating directly his fundamental opinion of the human experience than he does in this play. This opinion cannot be considered wildly optimistic. He makes no mention of a loving God. He does not posit a heaven; rather, death is inevitable and final. He does not deny that much of our daily world is cold and indifferent to us, and is permeated by evil and insanity. Weighing the good and the bad in life, Simon sees the scale tipping ever so slightly toward the good. What tips the scale is that some people, such as Barney, but not Elaine, try to comfort others as well as to find comfort for themselves.

Chapter Six

Loss and Recovery

The Gingerbread Lady

Despite the clear evidence in *Plaza Suite* and *Last of the Red-Hot Lovers* that Simon did not intend to spend the rest of his life writing soufflé comedies such as *Come Blow Your Horn* and *Barefoot in the Park,* many critics continued to regard Simon strictly as "a laugh machine." Simon once said, "I think people are quick to categorize *all* of my plays based on *some* of my plays. . . . I *don't* write the same play over and over." He specified, "I've tried to turn this whole thing around by flirting with danger a lot more. . . . I began trying things like *The Gingerbread Lady*—about an alcoholic former singer."[1]

The history of *The Gingerbread Lady* from its first rehearsal days to its opening night on Broadway is a history of Simon's attempt to write a comedy containing even more serious material than his two previous comedies did. In the original script, the third act was particularly somber. In his synopsis of Act Three, Richard Meryman wrote that Evy Meara, having been beaten up by her ex-lover, fought with her daughter and begged her ex-lover to take her to bed. Left alone, she proceeded to get drunk and to begin to maneuver Manuel, a street-smart Puerto Rican grocery boy, into bed with her. Meryman reported that while the play was still in rehearsals, Simon began rewriting the third act. "Simon lightened the first third of the last act—everything up to the humiliation scene with the ex-lover. Injecting laughter throughout, he made the daughter worriedly sympathetic and brought back Evy's dizzy friend Toby."[2] Nonetheless, this version of the play drew unenthusiastic reviews during its pre-Broadway run. Simon revised the play still more extensively.

In its final version, the play begins with Evy Meara's return to her apartment after a long stay in the sanitarium where she went after having gone on an alcoholic binge begun when her lover, Lou Tanner, jilted her.

While waiting for her, Jimmy Perry, a homosexual actor, pays Manuel for a supply of groceries. Evy comes in escorted by another friend, Toby Landau, a beautiful woman approaching her fortieth birthday. When Manuel returns with the rest of the order, Evy and he are mutually attracted to each other. After Toby and Jimmy leave, Evy's daughter Polly arrives. Polly's father, although no longer married to Evy, has acquiesced in Polly's desire to stay with her mother at least temporarily. Although Evy has reservations about such an arrangement, she agrees to give Polly's plan a trial run. Soon afterward, Lou Tanner appears, suggesting to Evy that they resume their relationship. Evy turns him down.

Three weeks later, Polly arranges a party to celebrate Toby's birthday. The party proves to be a fiasco. Jimmy has been fired by the producer of the play he was acting in, and Toby informs her friends that her husband is leaving her. Having bought champagne for the party, Evy, spurred by the unhappiness in her friends' lives and by her reawakened desire for liquor, becomes drunk and leaves for a rendezvous with Lou.

The next morning, Polly and Toby worriedly wait for Evy, who finally appears with a black eye given to her by Lou. Toby accepts the blunt truths Evy offers her—namely, that Toby should stop worrying about her fading beauty and focus her attention on her husband. After Toby leaves, Polly reminds Evy that Polly's father has arranged a luncheon for the three of them. Evy rebuffs Polly's suggestion that they keep the appointment, then tells Polly that they should stop living together. Hurt, Polly walks out. After Jimmy comes and goes, Polly returns. Realizing that Evy is about to begin another alcoholic binge, she pleads with her mother not to give in to self-destruction. Shaken by how unhappy Polly is, Evy agrees to try; she also agrees to let Polly stay on with her and to go with Polly to meet her ex-husband.

Although Simon's earlier plays have their flaws, none is as undercut by flaws as *The Gingerbread Lady* is. One problem is the first-act appearance of Manuel. The long exchange between Manuel and Jimmy contributes little information that is not presented more vividly elsewhere. The only important point conveyed during Manuel's conversation with Evy is that Evy's sexual appetite is far-ranging. This information, too, is amply indicated elsewhere. Nor is it important to establish Manuel as a character in order to prepare for his reappearance in Act Three, for in the final version of the play Manuel does not reappear in the third act. In sum, Simon, quite uncharacteristically, takes a tedious amount of time to build any momentum in Act One.

On the other hand, the first-act dialogue among Evy, Toby, and Jimmy effectively communicates how intensely insecure each of them is. Jimmy, for instance, is so nervous that when Toby—preceding Evy into the apartment by a couple of moments—appears, Jimmy asks, in a panic "How do I act in front of her?" Then he blurts out, "I'll kill her if she ever takes another drink."[3] Simon here, and even more powerfully in Act Two, dramatizes a sad paradox. Evy, Toby, and Jimmy are drawn to each other because of their desperate need for encouragement and strength and their recognition that the other two have the same need. In other words, they are attracted to weak people. Yet each hopes that the other two can somehow become strong and, in the process, make the third member of the trio strong, too.

Of course their wish can never come true. People who have been weak for so many years remain weak. Evy says to the other two, "When have you known me when I wasn't desperate?" (159). She has always been desperate, and what is true for her is true regarding the other two. Toby admits that she is obsessed with her looks, the symbol of her shallow values and her insecurity. Jimmy could not make himself go to the hospital to visit Evy, despite his love for her, because his ability to deal with the harsher aspects of reality is so tenuous.

Lou Tanner, Evy's ex-lover, is even more unstable and unreliable than the other three. He jilted Evy simply because he became momentarily infatuated with a younger woman. He wants to live with Evy again, but he admits how fruitless it would be for him to make Evy any promises of fidelity. He says that "in six weeks I may find another cute-assed little chick." He also tells Evy that "in eight weeks they might find you under the piano with a case of Thunderbird wine." Summarizing both their characters, he declares, "Together, Evy, we don't add up to one strong person. I just think together we have a better chance" (180).

Weak people, however, are less likely to lift each other up than to pull each other down. Simon astutely points out that these people are not entirely the victims of their weak natures. They are selfish. Although worried about Evy, both Toby and Jimmy concentrate on themselves. At the party, they are so absorbed in their sudden misfortunes that they are oblivious to the effect their emotional breakdowns have on Evy. So, too, Lou's desire to return to Evy is not inspired solely by his affection for her. Insolvent, he hopes Evy will once again feed and house and clothe him. More than that, his career as a songwriter has soured since he jilted Evy, and he as much as tells her he hopes that, by his living with her again, his career—stimulated by the intelligent criticism she occasionally gives him—will swing upward again.

Lou also establishes that Evy's love for him is more than a little selfish. He has to prod her into asking him about his career. He tells her that she "didn't give a damn if the stuff I wrote was good or not as long as it was finished. 'It's terrific, Lou, now come to bed'" (178). Evy's attempt to defend herself from this accusation merely validates Lou's attack. She says, "I had enough trouble getting affection from you without giving you bad reviews" (179). Evy, in fact, courts disaster even more intensely than her friends do. Evy drinks at the party not only when she listens to the misfortunes of Jimmy and Toby. She sneaks drinks every time no one else is watching her; and she had at least one drink before she came home. She later admits she drank on previous days as well.

Thus, it is Polly, not Jimmy, Toby, Lou, or Evy herself, who represents what hope there is that Evy can reverse the downward trend of her life. Simon's delineation of Polly, however, constitutes a far more serious flaw in the play than the first-act presence of Manuel. Polly is unconvincing, if not downright unbelievable, as a character. Quite simply, she is too good to be true. It is not impossible to believe that someone could be as nice as Polly; it *is* impossible to believe that anyone this side of sainthood could be that nice continuously. Polly is so wholesome she— although a seventeen-year-old New Yorker—is shocked by swear words. Polly is also continuously unselfish. As far as the audience can tell, Polly has no life of her own—no girls she pals around with or even talks to over the phone, no boy friends, no interests of any kind except her interest in her mother, to whom she wants to devote her whole life.

Nor is the audience ever given any indication how Polly became so nice, unselfish, optimistic, and strong. Her earliest years were certainly not filled with happy times, especially when Evy was around. If Polly grew up wholesome and happy, it was in no small measure due to her father. Yet Polly never concerns herself about her father. She never explains why she is so eager to deny him her love in order to be housekeeper for a mother who neglected her for increasingly longer periods of time. In Act Three she never explains why she wants to trick her father by helping to disguise Evy's beaten and alcoholically abused body. Stanley Kauffmann pinpointed another part of the basic implausibility of the situation when he stated, "We are asked to believe that Evy's ex-husband sends their daughter to live with his nymphomaniacal ex-wife just out of an alcoholics' hospital."[4]

Simon has never, in fact, created a thoroughly convincing preadult. The youngster in *The Goodbye Girl* is little more than the stereotyped "lovable" and "wise-cracking" kid seen in many other movies. Although an interesting character, Libby Tucker, the teenager in *I Ought to Be in*

Pictures, is also not totally believable. It is perhaps a good thing that Simon has rarely presented children or adolescents in his plays and movies.

Fundamental flaws overwhelm the play in the third act. Determined to have an upbeat ending, Simon deleted the reappearance of Lou and Manuel and brought Toby back into the spotlight. The audience is asked to believe that although Toby's marriage is threatened with total disintegration, self-centered Toby would spend her time not with her husband, Marty, or with a marriage counselor, but waiting for an alcoholic friend to come home from an all-night drunk. When Evy does appear, Toby says to her, "You've never had a lasting relationship with anyone who wasn't as weak or as helpless as yourself. So you have friends like Jimmy and me" (213). This valid insight intensifies the implausibility of what takes place next: Toby's complete about-face as a person. Evy tells her, "If you powdered Marty once in a while instead of your face, you'd be wearing *his* pajamas now instead of yours" (212). She adds, "You want to take some advice from a drunk? Go home, wash the crap off your face, put on a sloppy housedress and bring him a T-V dinner" (214). And that does the trick. Toby responds, "Wouldn't it be funny if you were right? . . . I suddenly hate my face. . . . I'm scared to death but I'm going" (214). That quickly, this woman who has been obsessed with her looks—with herself—for forty years now heads home a selfless woman.

Simon did strive harder to make plausible Evy's last-minute attempt not to go under completely again. The play stresses, for example, that Evy did turn things around in the sanitarium. Toby reports to Jimmy, "The doctors told me she worked harder than any patient there" (154). Dieting, Evy lost forty-two pounds. All this effort is verified by Polly. Her father, she tells Evy, spoke to Evy's doctor. Polly states, "He knows how hard you've been trying" (170). Back home, Evy also succeeds in resisting the temptation to resume her old way of life with Lou.

Nonetheless, Evy's achievements are just not outstanding enough to offset all the indications that she would resume her self-destructive pattern. Most of Evy's triumphs took place in a completely controlled environment—the sanitarium, which Evy describes as a prison. Evy pressured herself into achieving these triumphs in order to get out of that prison. So, too, as soon as she is home again she is such a bundle of nerves she can barely keep a grip on herself.

Add to this what did not happen at the sanitarium. Even with the encouragement of the doctors, Evy did not probe what led her to end up in the sanitarium. Toby asks Evy, "Didn't you learn anything in ten weeks at the hospital?" Evy replies, "The doctor tried to explain, but I was too busy making a pass at him." Then she asks, "If I knew, Toby, would it make any difference?" Toby replies, "It would help" (211); and she is, of course, right. Earlier, Toby asked Evy pointblank why Evy resumed drinking. In response, Evy said, "What do you want, a nice simple answer? When I was six years old my father didn't take me to the circus . . . How the hell do I know why I do anything?" (211). These are perfectly believable responses from someone who is going to keep drinking. They are not answers that portray a character on the threshold of achieving a fundamental personality reformation.

The same holds true concerning the minimal introspective journey Evy does allow herself to take. Polly, when worried about her mother, took a drink during the night in order to combat her throbbing headache. The next morning she tells Evy that the drink did not stop the throbbing, but it made it bearable. Then she asks, "Is that what it [drinking] does? Make things bearable?" (215). Evy says yes. Later, in an exchange with Jimmy, Evy describes Miss Havisham, the character in *Great Expectations* who, jilted on her wedding day, escaped reality by becoming a recluse. She tells Jimmy she feels she understands that woman.

That is as far as Evy's self-scrutiny goes: she drinks (and seeks sex) in order to escape. This analysis does not even convince Evy herself that she is going to reform, despite the support of the love Polly and she have for each other. That love cannot provide Evy with the strength or self-confidence she would need in order to turn her life around. Nor does Evy's milieu contain a host of other people who can help her gain strength. Barney in *Last of the Red-Hot Lovers* saves himself from melancholia by concentrating on Thelma, Jeanette, and himself. Thus, he is able to believe sincerely that at least a slight majority of people are decent. Barney's optimism is valid because even when he sees decent people such as Jeanette at their worst, these people are still self-disciplined and function successfully. Evy's life, on the other hand, is thickly populated with weak, self-destructive people such as Jimmy and despicable people such as the feckless Lou and the cruel producer of the play Jimmy is in.

Yet Evy would drink even if Toby and Jimmy did not come to her upset and depressed. A perceptive woman in many ways, she sees and is obsessed with every negative feature in the world around her. In this sense, she is like Elaine Navazio—but an Elaine Navazio ultimately out of control. Evy believes that if there is one chance in a hundred—and there always is—of something going wrong, it will go wrong; and she surrenders herself to that "inevitability." She considers that to do anything else is to live a lie, and she refuses to live that way. She "knows" she will fail again, a belief which ensures—and, for Evy, excuses—her failing again.

In the play's first two acts it is apparent that, in their relationship, Evy is the child and Polly is the parent. In Act Two, for instance, Polly cooks the dinner and is worried and annoyed when Evy does not come home at the scheduled time. Polly lectures Evy about Evy's unhealthy eating and sleeping habits because Polly assumes that all Evy needs in order to reform are a few "motherly" scoldings. When Evy becomes drunk, Polly realizes that her cheery belief Evy will climb steadily to health and happiness is an illusion. Polly, deeply shaken, announces she is "just plain sorry" (207) for Evy. Both Toby and Evy sense that the longer Evy and Polly live together, the less love Polly will feel for her mother.

The heroic, poignant high point in the play, therefore, is Evy's insistence that Polly return to living with her father. Evy tells Polly, "I just don't want to use you" (219). Evy accepts the company of Jimmy and Toby because they are like herself; but she wants Polly to do something better than try to fit her life into Evy's pattern of self-destruction. Polly yields to Evy's wishes and leaves.

Polly's return to the apartment—for a wallet she had forgotten to take with her—in the play's last scene is a blatantly obvious dramatic convenience. Suddenly, she decides that Evy wants her to go back to her father not because Evy is afraid of using Polly as a crutch or of destroying Polly's love for her, but simply because Evy is afraid to risk sincerely trying to reform. Just as suddenly, Evy decides that her love for Polly is so great she cannot resist her daughter's pleas that Evy not spend the rest of her life drinking. Evy resolves to try to do what Polly wants.

This ending, which is supposed to suggest that Evy might well succeed in turning her life around, is weak for the same reason, then, that the ending of The Odd Couple is weak. Evy is as vivid and clearcut a character as Oscar and Felix are. Thus, Simon was not free to manipulate Evy any way he wanted to merely to give his audience what it expected from his plays—an upbeat ending.

Commenting later on his having created a new ending for the play, Simon stated, "I'm sorry I did. I wish I had left it the other way."[5] He is right. In trying to have his cake and eat it, too—in trying, that is, to depict a basically unhappy person, yet provide that person's life with a happy ending—Simon spoiled his play.

The Prisoner of Second Avenue

Despite the difficulties Simon grappled with while creating *The Gingerbread Lady*, he stuck to his resolution to deal in comic fashion with features of the contemporary world which were not intrinsically comic. Describing how *The Prisoner of Second Avenue* originated, Simon told an interviewer, "I was very down on New York at that point, which is about when the taxi drivers started putting up those barriers between themselves and their passengers. It seemed to me symptomatic of what was going on in all our cities: People were so alienated and so fearful that they were separating themselves from contact. And not without cause. . . . I decided to make a statement about those urban ills and to do it in the form I write best: a comedy."[6]

The comedy takes place in the New York City apartment rented by Mel and Edna Edison. As the play opens, Edna discovers that in the wee hours of a sultry summer morning, Mel has gotten out of bed and is sitting in the living room, staring into space. When she asks him for an explanation, Mel ticks off many features of urban life that are bothering him. Ultimately Edna learns that Mel is deeply worried about the financial reversals the company he works for has suffered. In the next scene, Edna returns from shopping and finds the apartment has been burglarized. Entering soon afterward, Mel informs Edna that he has been laid off from work.

Edna quickly finds a job, but Mel becomes so despondent he has a nervous breakdown. His brother Harry and his three sisters meet in the apartment to discuss how much financial assistance they can give Mel. Edna asks that they contribute the money toward a down payment on a summer camp Mel could run. Mel's brother and sisters rebuff the suggestion—until Mel returns from his latest session with a psychiatrist. Shocked by his appearance and behavior, they agree to consider Edna's proposal.

Several weeks later, Harry returns with a check for the summer-camp project. Mel, however, has pulled out of his paranoiac depression. He tells Harry he can manage financially until he resumes work. Yet the Edisons continue to have problems. The business concern employing Edna has gone bankrupt. Furthermore, Mel's upstairs neighbor has twice doused water on Mel, and Mel now prepares to dump new-fallen snow on his neighbor's head.

Simon once remarked, "Mel and Edna in *The Prisoner of Second Avenue* are, in some respects, those kids from *Barefoot in the Park* 20 years later."[7] Paul Bratter grumbled about the apartment Corie had rented for them, but his basic personality was laced with enthusiasm, optimism, and energy. He shared Corie's love for the city and loved Corie as deeply as she loved him. Even when the two talked about getting a divorce, the audience realized it was witnessing a "lovers' quarrel." The situation with Mel and Edna, as Simon's comment implies, is quite different. Mel does not possess unlimited supplies of energy and enthusiasm, and he certainly is not optimistic about his or anyone else's future. His grumblings climb from dour grumpiness to paranoia. Nor does he play any lovers' games with Edna. He snaps at her—not because he is genuinely hostile to her, but because he is overwhelmed with exasperation. Yet Mel desperately needs Edna's love, and she, his. Their love for each other is vital to their efforts to maintain their sanity.

Still, although *The Prisoner of Second Avenue* tackles more serious contemporary problems than *Barefoot in the Park* did, its subject matter is dealt with quite superficially. The play is rich in funny lines. Thin in substance, however, and flawed in several other ways, it is not of the same quality as the three plays Simon wrote just before *The Prisoner of Second Avenue*. The first scene, for instance, is composed almost entirely of one-liners. It centers on Mel's responding at great length to Edna's opening question, "What's wrong?"[8] Mel complains about the summer heat, the malfunctioning air conditioner, the noise in the next door apartment, and many other matters. When he bangs on the wall, it cracks. He remarks, "It's a good thing I didn't try to hang a picture; we all could have been killed" (235).

The phrasing of the complaints is fresh and funny, but the scene contains almost nothing except topical complaints. There is no conflict. What could have compensated for the dearth of plot development is character development. But there is no character development, either. Mel is simply any urbanite who rails against his deteriorating environment. Edna is all patience; she is any wife who is sensitive to her husband's moods. That is all the audience learns about this couple.

Scene Two is better as the Edisons react to a specific and graphic grievance—the burglarizing of their apartment. Mel's opening line is one of the best in the play. Preoccupied with having just been fired from his job, he only gradually becomes aware of the chaotic condition of the apartment. Puzzled, he asks Edna, "Didn't Mildred come in to clean today?" (246). Their reactions to their mounting troubles are also of interest. Edna is now as upset as Mel was in the previous scene. First to enter the burglarized apartment, she hears but does not see Mel when he comes home. Thinking the burglars might have returned, she grabs a vase and is ready to do battle. Mel, on the other hand, is not yet ready to take action. He becomes introspective. Faced with financial hardship, he exclaims, "The garbage that we buy every year. . . . The food we never ate, the books we never read, the records we never played. Look at this! Eight and a half dollars for a musical whiskey pourer. *Eight and a half dollars!* God forbid we should get a little bored while we're pouring our whiskey! Toys! Toys, novelties, gimmicks, trivia, garbage, crap, HORSE-SHIT!!! . . . What did I give them twenty-two years of my life for? A musical whiskey pourer?" (256).

This is one of the moment-of-truth monologues Simon offers his audience in several of his plays. Although it does not strike as deep, it is similar to Sam's speech in *Plaza Suite* about wanting to achieve success all over again and Barney's speech in *Last of the Red-Hot Lovers* about his intense awareness that he, too, is going to die. Unfortunately, nothing else Mel says or does comes near to matching this moment of truth. He does not attempt to find any serious solution to his problems. Instead, preceding his mental collapse, he reverts to childhood, finding a mindless solace in playing softball with a group of young boys at a day camp.

The first scene of Act Two is another thin scene. Jobless, Mel is filled with an enervating anger. He has become still more meditative, but his musings lead him only to paranoia. He informs Edna that there is a "plot" at work, the "social-economical-and-political-plot-to-undermine-the-working-classes-in-this-country." Edna replies, "Oh, that plot." She begs him to hurry and name the "they" who are taking over everything. When Mel rants on, she says, "Mel, I've got to be in the office in twenty minutes. Please tell me who's taking over so I won't be late." (267).

The problem with these comments by Edna is that they are out of character. In the previous scenes, Edna was exceptionally sensitive to Mel's moods. One might say that in the present scene Edna, bursting with energy now that she is back in the business world, is too preoccupied trying to fix a meal on her lunch hour to be fully cognizant of Mel's mental condition, bizarre though that condition is. This explanation, however, is valid at most only for the first few moments of the scene.

Mel states that "the plot" has been created by "man undermining himself, causing a self-willed, self-imposed, self-evident *self-destruction*" (270). Having already presented the theme of self-destruction in *The Gingerbread Lady,* Simon might have explored the topic a little more now. He chose, instead, to have Mel veer into a tirade. Unfortunately, Mel's tirade, echoing all the ranting he did in the previous two scenes, is tedious.

Like the first scene of the play, the opening sequence of the next scene, featuring Mel's brother Harry and his three sisters, is funny as a set piece. With very little alteration, it could be presented separately to an audience, for no preliminary details about Mel's family were given in the earlier scenes. Simon himself later cited "the sudden introduction" of Mel's family as a flaw.[9] Their appearance is never made plausible. On the contrary, the audience is informed that not one of the four relatives has been invited to the Edisons' home in nine years. No explanation for this circumstance is offered, even though the audience learns that Mel is "the baby" of the family whom all the others have spoiled since he was born.

This scene is further undercut in two ways. The style of the scene is at variance with that of the rest of the play. The other scenes are presented realistically. This sequence is done in semi-absurdist, or Ring Lardner, style. Non sequiturs abound. A bigger problem focuses on Mel's personality. After stressing that the cause of Mel's breakdown resulted from forces outside Mel himself, Simon suddenly suggests that the root of Mel's woes lies solely within Mel's familial experiences. Brendan Gill elaborated on this point, noting, "We discover that what troubles Edison is not New York but who he is and has been and would have been had he been born in Galena or Prides Crossing: a fatherless Jewish boy with a mother and three sisters to dote on him and an elder brother to envy him in silence because it is Mel and not he who is the family favorite."[10]

In point of fact, Harry becomes a more interesting character than Mel. Harry's rueful references never to having been babied and to having had to carry the burden of family responsibilities long before he should have depict a poignant archetypal experience. One is eager to learn more about Harry, a desire intensified when Harry cajoles and coerces his sisters into helping Mel out financially. Harry exclaims, "I don't care what it's going to cost. The three of you can contribute whatever you think you can afford, *I'll* make up the deficit" (283). One senses that although Harry disapproves of the financial carelessness and waste in his brother's life, he is going to force himself to give a substantial amount of money to Mel and Edna because he feels guilty about being jealous of Mel.

In the final scene of the play, the sisters are barely referred to; they disappear from the Edisons' lives as abruptly as they appeared. Harry returns with a check for a summer camp, but he merely repeats the complaints he articulated earlier. Nothing more is made of the point. The idea of Mel's running a summer camp is a natural outgrowth both of his enjoyment of playing outside with youngsters and of his hostility toward urban life. Yet Mel now dismisses the idea of a camp. What he is interested in doing is never made clear.

Perhaps even more startling is Mel's quick mental recovery. After approximately two months of psychoanalytical treatment, Mel declares that he can do a more successful job of getting better on his own. (Characters in *Chapter Two* and *They're Playing Our Song* also imply they find psychiatrists of little help. Although Simon has said therapy helped him in his personal life, the indication in his plays is that people have to work out their problems without depending on professional guidance.[11]) Edna, on the other hand, has become extremely exasperated with city life. Where Mel previously bemoaned such things as the faulty air conditioner, Edna now bewails the temporary loss of running water when she so much wants to take a bath.

The final course of action that the Edisons pursue is, in mild form, similar to the one pursued by characters in Jules Feiffer's *Little Murders*. When the upstairs neighbor douses Mel with water a second time, the Edisons are galvanized into action. While earlier they settled for verbalizing their anger, now they let that anger direct their lives. They plan to fight back. They will dump snow on the head of their upstairs neighbor.

The sight of Mel and Edna sitting on the couch waiting for enough snow to fall to enable Mel to retaliate against his upstairs neighbor is another rich comic moment in the play. Yet, like the earlier comic moments, it does not hide the fact that *The Prisoner of Second Avenue* has a flimsy plot, a weak structure, and characters who only occasionally are more than one-dimensional. The play is little more than a series of very clever TV skits.

The Sunshine Boys

Jack Kroll stated that with *The Sunshine Boys* Simon "is back to his true form, the anthology of gags disguised as a play."[12] Actually Simon did something far more interesting. He blended the speech rhythms and point of view—and, sometimes, the jokes—used in the vaudeville routines performed by the play's two main characters, Willie Clark and Al Lewis, with the realistic story developed in the play. In *The Prisoner of*

Second Avenue, the sequence featuring Harry and his three sisters, although humorous, clashed stylistically with the rest of the play. The vaudevillian stylistic features permeating *The Sunshine Boys,* on the other hand, are quite fitting. The play focuses on two aging men who were in vaudeville for several decades. It is quite natural that vaudevillian speech patterns and a vaudevillian way of looking at life would have become ingrained in them. They effortlessly turn every episode in their lives into another vaudeville routine. Including one of the men's vaudeville skits in the play itself was a masterstroke on Simon's part. The skit is more than good fun; it dramatizes in a thoroughly delightful way just how completely such sketches came to dominate the way both Willie Clark and Al Lewis thought and spoke every day of their lives.

The plot begins with Willie's nephew Ben paying his weekly visit to Willie at Willie's New York apartment. Willie immediately criticizes Ben for not finding him some show-business work—even though it quickly becomes clear that Willie's failing memory prevents him from memorizing new lines. Ben informs Willie that a chance for Willie to work has arisen: a television network wants Willie and his now-retired partner, Al Lewis, to re-create one of their famous vaudeville routines as part of a show celebrating the history of comedy. At first Willie, still angry at his partner for retiring, rejects the proposal. Gradually, however, he allows himself to be talked into doing the show, although he insists on the need for rehearsals.

Ben arranges for a rehearsal to take place in Willie's apartment. When Willie and Al meet after an eleven-year hiatus, they almost immediately begin bickering. Willie finally badgers Al to the point where both men are shouting angrily at each other, and Al storms out of the apartment. Nonetheless, the two men meet at the television studio for one last run-through of the routine. Willie, however, has always resented Al's tendency to spit while enunciating certain words and to poke Willie too forcefully during the next turn in their routine. When Al does both these things during the run-through, Willie becomes uncontrollably angry and has a heart attack.

In the play's final scene Willie, in bed in his apartment, attempts and fails to make the nurse in attendance laugh. When Ben arrives, he tells Willie that the family cannot afford to keep paying for private nurses. Ben suggests two alternatives, and Willie chooses to retire to a home for actors in New Jersey. Al, upset because he was partially responsible for Willie's heart attack, comes to visit Willie. The two men start to bicker still again; but, in so doing, they begin quoting lines from another one of their old routines, and the tension eases. Both of them admit that they no longer have the energy to keep the feud going. Then Al confides that he will be leaving his daughter's home. It turns out he is going to take up residence in the same actors' home where Willie will be.

In terms of plot development, almost as little happens in the first scene of this play as in *The Prisoner of Second Avenue.* The audience learns that Willie wants to keep active in show business. Willie badgers Ben about getting him some work. Ben counters with the offer from the television studio. And that is it. The big difference between the opening scenes of the two plays is that in *The Sunshine Boys,* in addition to the plot development, a comparatively more complex—and far more interesting—man than Mel Edison is presented. For one thing, Willie insists that, although old, he is still a human being and therefore of some importance. He feels he deserves—and he tries to demand—respect. This facet of his personality is emphasized when Willie fights to be referred to as "Mr. Clark," not "Willie," by such people as the desk clerk at Willie's hotel. Entwined with this characteristic in Willie are Willie's pride and stubbornness. Willie refuses, for better and for worse, to let old age or other people humble him. His pride and stubbornness stop him from telling the desk clerk that the clerk—and not Willie himself—guessed correctly about what prevented Willie's television set from playing. For the same reason, Willie refuses to acknowledge the wisdom in the advice given to him by his nephew concerning the state of Willie's health and other matters.

Through the absorbing portrait he paints of Willie Clark, Simon stresses a theme pervading several of his plays—namely, the importance of each individual human being, young or old. In his very first play, *Come Blow Your Horn,* Simon humorously dramatized Buddy Baker's attempt to wriggle out from under his father's thumb and assert his individuality. *Barefoot in the Park* suggests people should complement—not duplicate—one another's personalities. The angry stance taken by Mel and Edna at the end of *The Prisoner of Second Avenue* indicates that they are not going to let the city run roughshod over them.

Willie's stubbornness and pride are the basis for the central point stressed from the start of the play: Willie's refusal to acknowledge he is an old man. He refuses to take care of himself. He eats the wrong foods, smokes cigars, and never exercises. When he learns that a show-business acquaintance, Sol Burton, has died at the age of eighty-nine, Willie spurns the possibility that age was a factor in Burton's death. It is Al Lewis's acknowledgment of age that particularly infuriates Willie. Al's fatigue had caused him to perform poorly when Willie and Al did one of their routines on an Ed Sullivan television show. That same night, Al had told Willie he was retiring from show business. Thus, Willie suddenly found himself without the partner he had worked with for forty-three years, a development that incensed him.

It is significant, too, though, that resentment had already been building up between the two performers—and building up in a way that was unavoidable. In actual theater history, there were several comedy-team partners who became so angry with each other they managed to avoid conflicts only by never speaking to each other except while on stage. Unfortunately, the first source of the increasing hostility between Willie and Al was bred by actions that occurred *during* their comedy acts. Al's habits of spitting his words out at Willie and of poking Willie too hard with his finger were linked with integral elements of their comedy routines.

Willie's cantankerousness soon shows itself in another way in Scene One. Previous to this day, Willie has been enraged at Al for breaking up the act; now, because of his hurt pride, he at first rejects the offer to work with Al even though Al is willing to do an old routine one more time. Pride leads Willie to claim that the only reason he yields to Ben's pressure to accept the offer is that, by yielding, he will promote business for Ben's theatrical agency. Al, too, incidentally, is not without pride or ego. In the play's second scene, Al emphasizes that the only reason *he* agreed to the reunion is that he wants his grandchildren to see him perform at least once in their lifetimes.

Like several other Simon characters, both men do give the family unit top priority. But there are, of course, other unacknowledged motives behind the two men's willingness to perform together again. For one thing, show business is in their blood. They hunger to perform. Willie also wants any show-business work he can get—if only to show the world that he can still perform professionally. Angry at Al, Willie would also like to show Al that there was no valid reason for their having broken up the act eleven years earlier.

One false note in the second scene is that it is unlikely that Ben, aware that Willie's resentment toward Al has been festering for years, would so soon leave the apartment where the two ex-partners have met to rehearse and let Willie and Al go at each other in whatever way they wish. Ben, in fact, states to Willie, "I'm going to stay until I think you're both acting like civilized human beings" (325). The two men, especially Willie, remain tense and wary of each other, yet Ben blithely departs all the same. The only other blemish in the play's first scenes is Simon's overfondness for the running gag. Willie's difficulty with the lock on his apartment door, for instance, is almost as overworked a gag as the one in *Barefoot in the Park* about the flights of stairs leading up to the Bratters' apartment. Willie's repeatedly kicking the cord for the television set out of its socket is another example. Yet even these vaudevillian "bits" advance the plot; they dramatize that Willie is aging.

What makes the second scene successful is that from the moment Al enters the apartment, it is abundantly obvious that, although old, he is a long way from being senile. He almost immediately jockeys Ben into using the same kind of vaudevillian speech rhythms and patter that Willie jockeys Ben into using. While listing his requests for props, Al shrewdly arranges to get himself a new suit. When Ben asks if Al has given him a complete list of the props, Al says yes. Willie immediately reminds Al about one more needed item; Al, without missing a beat and without acknowledging Willie's assistance, adds the one last item to the list. In sum, Al proves to be a match for Willie in any battle of wits.

Left alone, the two men are a hilarious study in stubbornness. Each wants the other one to be the first to admit he is eager to do the act again and is doing the act for personal satisfaction—not solely to please relatives. Willie, however, cannot contain his resentment. He repeatedly corrects the replica of the skit's set that Al creates. He insists they rehearse *his* way. When he suddenly also begins changing the script, Al explodes in anger. Willie instantly pounces on this outburst. He shouts, "You know why you retired? Because you were tired. You were getting old-fashioned. I was still new-fashioned, and I'll *always* be" (346). Although Willie does not admit it, his rebuttal reveals that he wanted a "reunion" with his partner in order to vent his anger at Al for Al's having retired.

What is not clear—and constitutes the only serious flaw in the play—concerns Al's provocative actions. Late in this first rehearsal scene, Al deliberately provokes Willie by poking Willie in the chest with his finger, an act that has always gotten Willie's goat. It is possible to explain Al's actions in this scene by saying he is merely retaliating to the needling and abuse Willie has aimed at him. But Al again deliberately provokes Willie while they are moving hilariously and smoothly through the final rehearsal of their skit in the television studio. There, Willie is first angered by Al's spitting. Al defends himself by saying, "I don't spit on purpose. I spit on accident. I've *always* spitted on accident. It's not possible to say that line without spitting a little" (364). Even if one accepts this explanation, there still remains the matter of Al's poking Willie again.

Why does Al poke Willie so hard when he could so easily have modified this "bit," gotten smoothly through the rest of the skit, and then performed the whole routine on camera for the benefit of his adoring grandchildren? Pauline Kael, discussing the film version, wrote, "We don't know where this calculated aggression comes from. . . . What was needed, I think, was for Lewis to turn into a different person as soon as he was rehearsing onstage—for something wild to break out of him, some domineering, manic charge."[13] Kael's specific suggestion, while possible for some other kind of performer, would not fit here. For Al states flatly in the play's final scene that it was Willie who was always too intense. Al declares, "You always took the jokes too seriously. They were just jokes" (388). Nonetheless, Kael is right in that some clue, some indication as to why Al provokes Willie is needed.

Simon's stage directions specify that one's *first* impression of Al is that he "is soft-spoken and pleasant" (328). Simon's presentation of Al's actions make it clear that Al harbors a great deal of anger, anger he unleashes slyly and with consummate effectiveness on Willie. But although Simon in other plays has deftly presented characters filled with anger—think of Elaine Navazio in *Last of the Red-Hot Lovers*—in this play he has failed to find a means of satisfactorily delineating a character who releases his deepest anger in a devious way.

After the comic peak of the vaudeville routine enacted in the first scene of Act Two, followed by the story's most dramatic moment—the heart attack Willie suffers as his rage mounts—it was inevitable that there be a dip in the play's intensity. Simon does not try to buck this inevitability. Yet he does not let the opening minutes of the play's final scene merely mark time. Reasserting the play's basic rhythm and point of view, Simon starts the humor on still another upswing in the exchanges between Willie and the nurse. More than that, Simon subtly indicates a basic change in Willie's life now that Willie has suffered a heart attack. Willie is accustomed to having his own way. Ben certainly has always yielded to him in the past. In this final scene, however, the nurse does not defer to him. Despite Willie's bullying banter, she remains in charge of the situation. This dramatizes that Willie's life is going to be irrevocably different from what it was before his heart attack.

Rebuffing his efforts to intimidate her, the nurse pressures Willie to acknowledge that his pride is by no means always an admirable quality. She tells him, for instance, that he cannot stand to let people do things for him. Later, she bluntly lectures him. She comments, too, that he never stops trying to get a rise out of people. Willie says, "When I stop, I won't be here." Without batting an eye, the nurse retorts, "Well, that's where you're gonna be unless you learn to slow up a little" (373). When Ben appears, he also lectures Willie. Significantly, Ben asserts himself much more forcefully with Willie than he ever did in the past. When Willie protests, Ben declares, "*I'll* decide for Willie Clark" (376). All of this leads to one of the most poignant moments in the play. Willie eventually agrees to go to the Old Actors' Home in New Jersey. Then he says to Ben, "I won't see you no more?" (379). For the first time, Willie admits how much he needs someone, needs company.

If Willie has finally mellowed, Al has mellowed even more. Simon believes in traditional moral values, especially concerning man's responsibility for his actions. So, like other Simon characters such as Alan Baker and Jeanette Fisher, Al suffers from a guilty conscience. Al is painfully aware he was wrong to provoke Willie deliberately. Al has lost weight and sent Willie candy and flowers.

Yet the two men do not fall into each other's arms as soon as they see each other. At first they scheme and bicker. Nonetheless, they indicate that they are ready to end the feud. They share a laugh over their automatically falling into the patter of another one of their old routines. Al admits to fatigue; and Willie, in another poignant moment, replies, "To be honest with you, for the first time I feel a little tired myself" (386).

Willie and Al will continue to argue with each other till their dying day. Their basic personalities, after all, are not angelic. But, if only because of their dwindling energy, they will not fight as frequently. Nor is Willie as hostile to Al as he was when Al first retired from show business. For Willie had used Al as a surrogate. Willie would not fight old age directly—that would have been to admit too much. Instead, he directed his rage about growing old at Al, who openly admitted he was aging. Now Willie will no longer fight with Al so vehemently because, despite his pride and stubbornness, Willie has begun to acknowledge he is an old man.

Discussing Willie and Al, Simon commented, "I spent my life growing up with these men. If they spoke in one-liners and punch lines instead of conversation, it's because it was the only language they knew."[14] This is why the many funny lines that Willie and Al speak are always an integral part of the play. Indeed, as far as Simon's full-length plays are concerned, this comedy is his tightest in structure. Every turn in every scene adds to the play as a whole. Despite its imperfections, *The Sunshine Boys* constitutes Simon's most skillful theater work to date.

Chapter Seven
Deeper into Movies
Three Films

During the 1970–1972 period that *The Gingerbread Lady, The Prisoner of Second Avenue,* and *The Sunshine Boys* reached Broadway, Simon continued to write screenplays. Two of his film-scripts were his latest adaptations of his plays. Simon's scripts took no serious advantage of the possibilities, visual or otherwise, that movies had to offer. Instead, to an even greater extent than his earlier adaptations, these scripts transferred the plays' material to the screen with dull fidelity. They offered the moviegoer "photographed plays."

The movie version of *Last of the Red-Hot Lovers* was not particularly successful. Even the critics who liked the film were just mildly enthusiastic. Quite rightly, only Alan Arkin's performance as Barney Cashman drew much applause. Sally Kellerman gave the poorest performance of the three leading women. Her attempt at laconic underplaying made it appear that Elaine Navazio was simply a bored housewife.

Plaza Suite, which preceded *Last of the Red-Hot Lovers* to the screen, generated even less praise. Arthur Hiller's direction was heavy-handed, but perhaps the foremost flaw was the acting. In the play, as a kind of acting tour de force that playgoers are used to seeing, George C. Scott had played all the lead male roles and Maureen Stapleton all the female leads. Confusing the movie audience more than a little, three different leading women appeared in the film while Walter Matthau, sometimes sporting hair styles that looked like distractingly ridiculous wigs, played the three male roles. Worse, as Sam Nash and Jesse Kiplinger, Matthau floundered beyond his range as a performer. Nonetheless, some of the blame for the blandness of the movie belongs to Simon. He himself later admitted he was not pleased with his scripts for *Plaza Suite, Last of the Red-Hot Lovers,* or *The Prisoner of Second Avenue.* Simon confessed, "I really didn't have an interest in films then. I was mainly interested in continu-

ing writing for the theater. . . . The plays never became cinematic."[1]
Nevertheless, Simon was moving deeper into movies, for during this
period he wrote two original screenplays. The first was *The Out-of-
Towners*. He had first considered using the material as part of the play
Plaza Suite. Actually, in its dramatization of Simon's irritation with New
York City, *The Out-of-Towners* resembles *The Prisoner of Second Avenue*
more than it does *Plaza Suite*.

The Out-of-Towners

The main characters in *The Out-of-Towners*, George and Gwen Keller-
man (played by Jack Lemmon and Sandy Dennis), fly from Dayton,
Ohio, to New York as part of the procedure by which George is slated to
become in New York a vice president in charge of company sales. The
Kellermans plan to spend a gala evening on the town, retire to their hotel
room, and then rise in time for George to go to his interview before they
return temporarily to Dayton. At the last minute, however, their plane is
rerouted to Boston. Once there, George, determined to have his night on
the town anyway, convinces Gwen they should take a train to New York.
Because of the crowded conditions in the coaches, the train ride proves
very uncomfortable. Arriving late, the Kellermans discover that New
York is in the throes of multiple labor strikes. With no taxis available,
they finally reach their hotel only to find that their reservation was
canceled by the management because of their tardiness. After they leave
the hotel with a stranger who has offered them sympathy and aid, the
stranger robs them. Seeking help from the police, the Kellermans are put
in a car headed for an armory where they can sleep; then the police car is
hijacked, and the Kellermans are dumped in Central Park.
The next morning, they are robbed again, and George is roughed up.
Later, in his attempt to reach his interview, he manages to hitch a ride,
but the car, owned by a diplomat, is attacked by demonstrators. George
decides that he does not want the New York City job after all. Gwen
heartily endorses his decision. The couple board a Dayton-bound plane
which is hijacked and forced to head for Cuba.
Presented skillfully, the ever-mounting series of misfortunes could be
hilarious—somewhat unbelievable, but hilarious. In the film, however,
these misfortunes become merely mind-numbing. What partially accounts for this is the film's governing style. Instead of shaping the material
in at least semifarcical fashion, the director, Arthur Hiller, insisted on

strictly realistic format. Consequently, all too often the audience sighs or moans rather than smiles at the Kellermans' tribulations. There are other basic weaknesses. The Kellermans, particularly George, tiresomely go out of their way to court disaster. It becomes increasingly difficult to tolerate—never mind laugh at—George's bull-headedness. More than once, Simon's script introduces characters who show the audience that the Kellermans could do the sensible thing instead of the foolish thing. One man who also was sidetracked when the plane was rerouted to Boston, for instance, simply slept over in comfortable Boston accommodations and reached New York the next morning. The Kellermans never do the obvious, sensible thing.

But the biggest flaw in the film is George Kellerman. He is basically an unpleasant—to say nothing of unfunny—fellow. Arthur Knight accurately described George as "a chronic, compulsive worrier, more than a bit of a bully, short-tempered, vengeful, and pigheaded."[2] When his wife suggests any alternative to one of his plans, despite the admirable practicality of her proposal, George always loudly intimidates her into accepting his plan. George also becomes increasingly vindictive— often threatening to get whomever he is dealing with in deep trouble even when that person is not responsible for George's misfortunes. Roger Greenspun incisively summed up George when he wrote, "Simon has inexplicably created a hero more offensive than, say, the New Haven Railroad—which is a coup of sorts, but not one that many comic dramatists will care to emulate."[3]

The film's defects irreparably harm what might otherwise have been a comedy with an interesting serious point. For George and Gwen Keller-man, like Mel and Edna in *The Prisoner of Second Avenue,* protest against dehumanizing contemporary conditions. Although the Edisons talk more than once about buying a camp in a rustic setting, they do not leave their urban environment; but they do rebel and, in their screwy way, prepare to fight for their dignity and self-preservation. The Kellermans rebel still more firmly. They refuse to move to the "big city," although the refusal costs George a top company position. The film's criticism of the urban world is rendered toothless, however, because the audience remains unconvinced that the Kellermans' woes were not to a large extent their own fault.

The Heartbreak Kid

Based on Bruce Jay Friedman's short story "A Change of Plan," but altered and extensively elaborated on, *The Heartbreak Kid* is the best film created thus far from a Neil Simon script. Starring Charles Grodin and Jeannie Berlin as the honeymooners, the film opens with the first meeting between Lenny Cantrow and Lila Kolodny, their whirlwind courtship, and their traditional Jewish wedding. While on their way to a Florida honeymoon, Lenny realizes that Lila has a host of little habits and traits that quickly douse his romantic ardor for her. The first day on the beach in Miami, Lila gets a horrendous sunburn and is forced to stay in her hotel room for days. During this period, Lenny becomes entranced with the beauty and teasing manner of Kelly Corcoran, played by Cybill Shepherd.

Inventing melodramatic stories to keep Lila from becoming suspicious, Lenny joins Kelly and her parents at their nightclub table, spends a day sailing with them, and soon afterwards inform Kelly's parents that he wants to marry Kelly. Lenny takes Lila out to dinner and tells her he wants a divorce. Within a week, Lenny has instigated divorce proceedings and driven to Minnesota, the Corcorans' home state. There, he wins Kelly away from her college admirers and seduces her in her family's woodland cabin. Kelly successfully pleads with her father to invite Lenny to dinner. After the meal, Mr. Corcoran attempts to induce Lenny into abandoning his pursuit of Kelly. Lenny remains adamant and ultimately weds Kelly. The wedding reception shows, however, that Lenny has still failed to win over Mr. Corcoran and his friends. Lenny ends up talking aimlessly to two young kids, who just stare at him.

In this script Simon achieves his goal of creating humor out of situations which are not basically surefire comedy material. So, too, almost nothing said in the film could be described as a one-liner. The humor emanates from the characters. Occasionally these characters are too awful to laugh at comfortably. But what gives the film its unique flavor is that usually the characters are "just awful enough" to elicit the audience's laughter.

A perfect case in point is Lila. The whirlwind courtship takes place in an atmosphere that dulls both Lila's and Lenny's perceptions in the same way that soft-focus camera shots haze some pictures' romantic interludes. Lila does not see what a demanding and egotistical man Lenny is. Lenny fails to look closely at Lila. This mutual blunder is highlighted when Lenny starts unzipping Lila's skirt in order to have sex with her. She demurs, asking him to wait until their wedding night. Lenny, much to his later regret, chivalrously yields to Lila's wish. If Lenny had pursued his desire for sex, he might well have come "to know" Lila both sexually and in terms of her personality; Lila, too, might have seen Lenny in more realistic terms. They might then, in turn, have slowed their romance down a bit because of the doubts their insights bred—or they at least might have begun their honeymoon less starry-eyed, less vulnerable to disappointment. As Stephen Farber commented, "Lenny and Lila don't know anything about each other when they get married, but they think they're 'in love.' "[4] As Lenny and Lila drive south, they start singing. Lenny blurts out, "You have the lousiest voice." The grating quality in her singing voice is one of the first "little things" that displeases Lenny and that ultimately leads to his final dissatisfaction with Lila. At the time, however, it is her reply to his criticism that jolts him. She pugnaciously retorts, "You'll just have to get used to it." The pugnaciousness itself dismays him, but not as much as his realization that if they stay married, he will indeed have to live with all her imperfections—an increasingly repelling prospect for a perfectionist such as Lenny.

Now, Lenny takes a steady look at Lila, who proceeds to display other "little habits" that make the audience chuckle, but that fill Lenny with dismay. She wants immediate and precise praise for her every sexual performance. She insists Lenny repeatedly tell her that sex with her is "wonderful." Her sense of humor is vulgar; she thinks it funny to expose her breast to a truck driver passing Lenny and herself on the highway. Already on the hefty side, she consumes what seems like a carton of Milky Ways a day. She loves egg-salad sandwiches so much that when she eats one, she ends up with bits of egg sprinkled all over her face.

Yet no central character in the film becomes a caricature. Simon could easily have used Lila's petty vulgarities as a means of making her completely ridiculous, thus encouraging the audience to sympathize with Lenny completely. This, however, would have been a bad mistake; for then the obvious question would arise as to how during their courtship could even a starry-eyed Lenny have failed to see Lila as she is. Simon did not want Lila to be wholly unappealing. (In fact, he tried, but failed, to have the attractive Diane Keaton cast as Lila.) As gauche as Lila is, she is not a mere buffoon. She explains her desire for instant sexual praise by saying shyly, "I have to be reassured," revealing a lack of confidence beneath her brashness. When Lenny and she bicker, she is the one who, kissing him gently, tries to ease the situation. While in a restaurant, they see a gray-haired couple helping each other put on their coats. Lila says wistfully, "That's going to be us."

Lenny replies, "Is it?" He has already silently begun to question whether he will put up with Lila's unappealing traits for the rest of his life. When Lila's sunburn confines her to their hotel room, he relishes this unexpected chance to be free of her and to seek out the young woman he has already become enamored of. For if Lenny was starry-eyed when he first met Lila, he is sunlight-dazzled when he first meets Kelly Corcoran. Lying on the beach, he looks up at her, and the sunlight, cascading down her lovely blonde hair, makes her look like a golden goddess—the embodiment of all his romantic daydreams. Later, he tells her, "I've been waiting for you all my life." He is continually dazzled by her. Soon after he arrives in Minnesota, she takes him to a woodland cabin her family owns. Lenny sees this, too, as a fulfillment of his dreams. He declares, "All my life I wanted to be in a place like this with a girl like you."

It is not impossible to believe that Lenny could fall blindly in love with Lila because he does exactly the same thing with Kelly. It is true that Kelly, whatever her faults, is at first glance much more attractive than Lila. But that is not the point. The point is that Lenny's moods shift drastically and that each mood greatly alters his perception of the world—of the women—around him. When emotionally sober, he can be an extremely hard-to-please perfectionist. At other times, when the sentimental side of his nature gains full reign, he drifts far away from reality. Indeed, one insight highlighted by the movie is that a perfectionist and a sentimentalist can constitute two sides of the same coin. So, too, one can reinforce the other.

Proof of Lenny's romantically sentimental nature can be seen repeatedly during the early dialogue between Lenny and Kelly. She makes several innocuous comments which Lenny laughs at as if she had ad-libbed the cleverist witticisms of all time. At one point in their conversation Lenny asks her what she is thinking. She says, "How do you expect me to think when I'm listening?" Instead of giving Lenny pause, this reply renders him giddy with laughter. On another occasion, he says, "Where'd you get that laugh?" and fails to reflect on the loaded implications embedded in Kelly's response, "My father bought it for me." Nor does he perceive the tougher side of her nature when she keeps needling him about his "cute little wife" or when, after he first tells her that he is married, she blithely comments, "So what else is new?"

Totally wrapped up in his adoration of Kelly, Lenny is unaware that she is flip about his marital status because she does not take her vacation "romance" with Lenny very seriously. She *is* attracted to Lenny, who is so different from all the WASP males she has known. (It is interesting that Simon did not want Lenny's Jewishness featured in the film despite the fact that its inclusion adds another whole dimension to the attraction Lenny and Kelly feel for each other.) Nonetheless, the Florida "romance" is basically unreal to Kelly. It is merely an amusing game. She is not deeply emotionally involved. Lenny asks her, "What would you do if your dad told you to drop me?" She answers, "Drop you." She toys with Lenny. Lenny, for instance, pleads for time to extricate himself from his marriage, a task that will necessitate his dropping "a bombshell" on Lila. Kelly, enjoying his dilemma, increases the pressure on him. She forces him to go sailing all day with her even though this will intensify his need to hit Lila with "a bombshell." Kelly simply comments, "Bombs away." Vincent Canby aptly defined Kelly as "lovely, bitchy and funny, all more or less simultaneously."[5] Lenny changes himself for Kelly's benefit. He wears his hair the way she wants him to. He begins to dress as conservatively as her father. Yet Kelly promises him nothing. Pressed for a commitment, she says not a word. Lenny's giddy response to this is, "That look in your eye is enough for me."

Lenny remains undaunted. Aware of Mr. Corcoran's hostility toward him, Lenny rises to the challenge. He tells Kelly, "Don't underestimate me." This sets up one of the funniest scenes Simon has ever written: Lenny tells Kelly's parents of his present marital predicament and his desire nevertheless to marry their daughter. For a long time, the parents sit in stunned, silent disbelief—and who could blame them? Lenny informs them that his plan to marry Kelly is hindered by a "slight complication"—he is on his honeymoon. He proceeds to explain that his current wife is not really his "type." Trying to reassure them, he goes on to say he married Lila only because he thought "it was the decent thing to do," but he now realizes "decency doesn't pay off."

All the while, Kelly sits munching pretzels and staring into space, as remote from the immediate scene as a Greek goddess sunning herself on Mount Olympus. Nor is Lenny disconcerted when Mr. Corcoran (played by Eddie Albert), finally managing to find his voice, describes his vehement, scathing condemnation both of Lenny's plan to marry Kelly and of Lenny himself. Lenny comments, "That's an honest answer." He summarizes Mr. Corcoran's remarks by stating, "What you're saying is: If I want Kelly, I'm going to have to put up a hell of a fight." This, of course, was not what Mr. Corcoran said at all.

The first thing Lenny must do is break the bad news to Lila. The restaurant scene in which he does so is a curious mix. Some of it is quite funny. In his attempt to put Lila into the right frame of mind, for instance, Lenny nervously spouts a string of vague platitudes. He reminds Lila that she, being young, has her whole life before her, and that everyone has to learn from whatever happens to him in life. She exclaims, "I never knew you were so deep." He speaks of the need to prepare for anything, and that she deserves something better than the bad break that has come to her. She interprets this to mean that Lenny has discovered he is dying.

Sweating profusely because he "feels the heat" in the restaurant, Lenny blurts out, "I'm not dying. I want out of the marriage." From this point on, the comic element in the scene fades away. The rest of the scene is distinctly without humor; it also goes on for much too long a time. Lila, shocked, feels sick to her stomach. She pleads with Lenny to give her a quarter so that she can go to the ladies' room. Lenny, intent on trying to calm Lila down, keeps refusing to let her get up from the table. Although their waiter had informed Lenny the restaurant is out of pecan pie, the desert Lila requested earlier in the meal, Lenny bullies the waiter into searching for a piece of pecan pie for her. Now, when the waiter brings the pie, Lenny, feeling guilty, becomes preoccupied with trying to coax the nauseated Lila into eating it.

Because no situation in the last segment of the film, taking place in cold Minnesota, matches the craziness of a young man falling in love with one woman while on his honeymoon with another woman, the rest of the movie never reaches the comic heights scaled in the sunny Florida segment. The transitional scenes, including Lenny's meeting with his lawyer to begin divorce proceedings, are nothing but transitional scenes. Kelly is nudged to some degree out of her bemused attitude toward Lenny by his actually having pursued her to Minnesota. She simplemindedly states, "I'm really flattered you came here." Still, she soon tells him she has to hurry to her English Lit class. Stunned, Lenny emphatically declares that what has been going on between them is "no game." But this potentially rich scene is filmed outdoors on Kelly's college campus and is badly undercut by the distracting noise and the hustle and bustle of students hurrying to their classes. Lenny and Kelly have to shout to be heard and have to converse in the bland presence of Kelly's WASP male admirers, who stand at her side.

Nonetheless, Kelly is now truly impressed by the forcefulness of Lenny's character. She hastens to explain that he has caught her "off guard." She pleads with him to give "a girl a chance." The next main scene, however, in which Lenny intimidates Kelly's male admirers into backing out of the competition for Kelly, is the weakest scene in the movie. It occurs amid the same distracting hustle-and-bustle atmosphere surrounding the reunion between Lenny and Kelly. Worse,

Lenny's sudden pretense—in order to scare off Kelly's boyfriends—that he is a narcotics agent is totally unconvincing; they already know who Lenny is.

The film picks up in momentum when Lenny and Kelly are alone in her parents' cabin. More and more genuinely intrigued by Lenny, Kelly opens up to him emotionally. This is symbolized by the last "game" she instigates—a game in which they are to strip and stand close to one another, but not touch. For the final time, Lenny pushes their relationship beyond a "game." Although Kelly states she will not sleep with him, Lenny—stung by the unhappy results from his having postponed sex with Lila—succeeds in seducing Kelly. A few days later, Lenny is invited to the Corcoran home, for Kelly is now fascinated by him. He had mesmerized Lila with his talk, and he does the same thing with Kelly, who exclaims, "I love listening to you." Significantly, his forcefulness reminds her of the only other man she loves—her father.

Lenny is, in fact, not the only one to gaze at Kelly through a romantic filter. While Lenny sees her as a goddess, Mr. Corcoran sees her as a child-virgin. He still considers her his "baby." This is why, when she gets on her knees and pleads with him to invite Lenny to dinner, and touches him literally and emotionally, Mr. Corcoran relents; like Lenny, he yields to the woman of his dreams.

When, after dinner, Lenny tells Mr. Corcoran that he wants Kelly, Mr. Corcoran shouts, "So do I, goddam it." This possessive love, in the best comic scene in the latter part of the film, triggers Mr. Corcoran's desperate, semihysterical attempt to bribe Lenny to leave his daughter alone. Mr. Corcoran tries so hard—and so woefully in vain. Lenny interrupts, to point out the anti-Semitism in Mr. Corcoran's angry words and to speak proudly of spending years in the war fighting against such bigotry—although he ultimately admits he was actually nowhere near the front lines. Mr. Corcoran's crudity and selfishness also make Lenny, by comparison, more appealing. Perhaps Lenny's finest moment occurs when Mr. Corcoran keeps upping the amount of money he will give Lenny if Lenny will go away. Lenny, sincerely upset, states, "I didn't come out here to *negotiate* for Kelly."

Originally, the wedding reception for Lenny and Kelly constituted the penultimate, not the final, sequence in the film; and it could be argued that the original last sequence—in which Lenny on his second honeymoon becomes aware that Kelly has *her* share of annoying habits—is necessary in order to bring home the point that Lenny's desire for perfection is going to cause much unhappiness in his second marriage. But the whole film indicates this major facet of Lenny's personality. The second wedding reception is much less festive and joyous, much more subdued than the first. It is poignantly clear that Lenny, having climbed his social Mount Everest (that is, having married a WASP beauty), is all alone up there. At first, Lenny talks with various friends and relatives of the Corcorans, but he elicits no warm response. Reciting opinions he has just read in the newspaper, Lenny reveals still more fully his basic shallowness. He has no serious interest in any vocation or avocation. The audience knows, too, that he has married a prettily wrapped package containing nothing inside.

The last moments of the film stir sadness; for, drained of energy and feeling a little bewildered and lost, Lenny ends up spouting more shallow comments to his only remaining listeners, two staring kids. He becomes vaguely aware of a "falling off." Learning that the boy listening to him is ten years old, Lenny murmurs that he, too, was ten once.

The film is so rich in content that it touches on several themes Simon's plays had already sounded. The adolescent selfishness of Lenny, Lila, and Kelly contrasts with the movement toward maturity on the part of Alan Baker—and even Buddy Baker—in *Come Blow Your Horn*. That Lenny is an extreme perfectionist and sentimentalist separates him from *Barefoot in the Park*'s Paul and Corie Bratter, both of whom learn and accept that moderation is best. Like Jesse Kiplinger and Muriel Tate in *Plaza Suite*, Lenny and Lila wrap themselves in illusions. Depleted and deflated at the end of the film, Lenny dramatizes a theme in all three segments of *Plaza Suite*—namely, that winning the goal is no guarantee of happiness. Finally, where Barney Cashman in *Last of the Red-Hot Lovers* opted ultimately to do the decent thing, Lenny pursues his wildest daydreams and, unlike Barney, causes considerable pain, anguish, and disillusionment.

Chapter Eight
Back on Broadway
The Good Doctor

On 17 July 1973 the *New York Times* reported that Joan Baim Simon, Neil Simon's wife, had died of cancer. Simon was emotionally devastated, so devastated that he was unable to deal directly with Joan Simon's death in his writings for a long time. That same year, however, he met Marsha Mason, the woman who became his second wife and the model for Jennie, a character in Simon's autobiographical play *Chapter Two*. They met during the auditions for the first Simon play to appear after Joan Simon's death, *The Good Doctor*. This play represented quite a change of pace for Simon. Looking back on its genesis, he said, "I started to write a Russian farce, but I didn't think it would hold for a whole evening. Then I read Chekhov's 'The Sneeze,' and I got excited. I decided it would have to be on stage. But what do you do with a 15-minute story?"[1] Simon read over a hundred stories by Chekhov before finding enough material to adapt for an evening of theater.

Despite some misgivings, Simon liked the idea of forsaking his usual format. *The Good Doctor* was his first straight play that did not have a New York setting or any New York characters. During the tryout period, Simon was made even more aware of this play's stylistic departure from the norm. He later reported, "When the play was being performed in New Haven, I remember a woman coming up to me during intermission and saying, with a dour look on her face, 'It's not Neil Simon.' I asked her if that meant the play was good or bad, and she said, 'I don't know. It's just not Neil Simon.' She had come to expect something else."[2]

The title, *The Good Doctor,* is a play on words. It refers to Chekhov, who was a doctor as well as writer, and to Simon himself, whose nickname is "Doc." The lead character is the Writer, about whom Simon commented, "He could be one of many people—either Chekhov or the writer Trigorin in 'The Seagull' or me."[3] By means of his portrait of the

Writer, presented mainly in the play's opening and closing monologues, Simon defines the archetypal writer. The Writer would rather talk than write because talking is easier to do. The Writer knows, too, he cannot escape feeling that "life is passing"[4] him by, that while he merely writes about life, other people "live." Yet he realizes that brooding about this is a waste of time, for he will not talk the day away or stop writing in order to "live." He will write because writing is a compulsion with him. Indeed, even when he is talking to someone, he is working at his craft. The Writer states, "All the time I'm thinking, 'He'll make a wonderful character for a story'" (393). So, too, the archetypal writer is a perfectionist who, reading his work in print, sees "that it's all wrong, a mistake, that it ought never to have been written" (393). The Writer has also come to expect to be compared to some other writer who is always pronounced his superior. Sometimes, full of regret and exasperation, the Writer daydreams about what he would do if he did not concentrate on writing. He comments, "I would like to tell you what I would most like to do with my life. Ever since I was a small child, I always" (394)—but then an idea for still another story occurs to him, and he becomes sidetracked. Not until the end of the play does the Writer recall what he wanted to do with his life when he was still a child. It was: to write.

This concise definition of a writer is charmingly presented. What gives it an extra dimension is that Simon makes the Writer's monologue quite autobiographical. In his introduction to *The Comedy of Neil Simon,* Simon, like the Writer, describes himself as primarily an observer (which is also what Corie "accuses" Paul of being in *Barefoot in the Park*). Even when he is a participant in some tense situation, he is always simultaneously making mental notes, viewing that situation from a neutral vantage point. Simon is also a perfectionist; he relishes the chance to revise his work over and over. Finally, by means of the Writer, Simon was able to express his own periodic exasperation with a public that, like the dour-faced woman at the New Haven tryout, does not want him to try anything different even though, if he keeps writing the same kind of play, he will be compared to some other writer and judged inferior.

Because this play is a distinct departure from Simon's earlier theater efforts, one wants Simon's artistic courage to be rewarded with artistic success. The playlets that constitute *The Good Doctor,* however, are not often very good. Many of the sketches in the first half of the piece are weak work. "The Sneeze," the sketch that immediately follows the Writer's first monologue, is a case in point. It centers on a government clerk named Cherdyakov who, while at the theater, accidentally sneezes on the man he works for, General Brassilhov. He immediately apologizes. Then, becoming convinced that the General will seek revenge for being sneezed upon, the next day the panic-stricken Cherdyakov apologizes again to his superior. Later, he becomes furious with himself for apologizing so abjectly, shouts insults at the General, and dies of emotional exhaustion and mortification.

Simon quickly dramatizes Cherdyakov's preoccupation with the social hierarchy and with his trying to better himself socially. Simon makes it clear Cherdyakov and his wife buy theater tickets for seats in a more prestigious section than the people of Cherdyakov's status would normally occupy. In this sense Cherdyakov, like so many other Simon characters, pays for his transgressions. He is punished for trying to rise above his proper station; for if he had been seated among his social equals, the sneeze would not have caused him more than a moment's embarrassment. Cherdyakov is also punished because of his ego, which leads him to assume the General is brooding about Cherdyakov when, in reality, the General completely forgot about the theater incident moments after it occurred.

Simon makes Cherdyakov humorously ridiculous in the initial theater scene, but he does not intensify Cherdyakov's obsession with social stature thereafter. Nor does Simon convincingly present Cherdyakov as someone who would, after abjectly apologizing, suddenly become as rebellious as a revolutionary. Simon also fails to establish early in the skit any physical instability in Cherdyakov that would make his sudden death less of a complete surprise.

The next three sketches are even slighter. "The Governess" is a monotonous piece in which a mistress of an estate relentlessly bullies a governess out of most of the salary she has earned. Then the mistress, after scolding the governess for not battling harder for her rights, gives her the full amount of money she deserves. The whole skit turns on the faint smile that appears on the governess's face as she takes the money—a smile that startles the mistress into wondering if the servant did not deliberately let herself be bullied, knowing that the mistress would then reverse herself in precisely the way she did. Although slyly suggesting that the "powerless" lower class is shrewd, and therefore not completely powerless, this twist in the story is too brief and too long in coming to justify the monotony of the dialogue that precedes it.

In "Surgery" Simon endeavors to deal comically with human pain. In farcical fashion, he presents the attempt of the inexperienced assistant of a village dentist to extract a tooth paining a patient. Unfortunately,

"Surgery" is a belabored piece. Edythe M. McGovern accurately described it as "a rehash of an old vaudeville routine."[5] Jack Kroll was particularly disappointed that the sketch shunned the social overtones in Chekhov's original story, which satirized "the callous pomposity of a flunky who wreaks havoc by trying to imitate his superiors."[6] After "The Sneeze" and "The Governess," none of the play's material includes any incisive social-political level of meaning. "Too Late for Happiness," a musical sequence, features two shy elderly people who, meeting by chance in the park, suppress their desire to develop a relationship despite their awareness they will live only a short time longer. It is a poignant moment, but the slightest piece of writing offered in *The Good Doctor*.

The last playlet in the first act is "The Seduction." This sketch is a lengthy one involving Peter, a Russian Don Juan, who strives to gain sexual favors from the wife of an acquaintance. Peter prides himself on winning many wives' affection after engaging in but one brief face-to-face encounter with the ladies. It is a clever enough idea for a playlet, but Simon does not do all that much with it, especially in the many segments leading up to the climax. The main problem is that Peter, in explaining his method of seduction, does far too much talking. His chatter becomes repetitive and sidetracks the audience from the comparatively more interesting, and far more dramatic, element in the story—namely, the wife's pretending to disapprove of Peter each time her husband comes home to report his latest conversation with Peter. The dim-witted, complacent husband remains oblivious to his wife's increasing fascination with Peter, who, in every conversation with the husband, praises her virtue and beauty ever more ardently.

In order for its flaws to be outweighed decisively by its virtues, the skit needs a resounding effective climax. None is provided. The wife arranges to meet Peter alone and tells him he may do with her whatever he wishes, but that if he admires her, instead of just lusting for her, he will not take advantage of her compliance because to do so would wreck her whole life. Peter lets her return to her husband a faithful wife. This plot twist falls flat. For here again, as was the case concerning Cherdyakov in "The Sneeze," Simon fails to do something vitally necessary to make his adaptation carry the day: he fails to convey convincingly a Russian temperament given to sudden extreme reversals in behavior. Nor does Simon indicate earlier in the plot anything else in Peter's character that would serve as an explanation for his abrupt about-face. Peter did not become a notorious seducer of women—and it is made clear that he is one—by turning sentimental and letting all his women return to their husbands untouched. Yet that is precisely what he does in this situation. Thus, the ending of "The Seduction" appears contrived and overly sentimental.

Three out of the four sketches comprising Act Two are, to varying degrees, stronger work. The one mediocre skit is "A Defenseless Creature." As in "Surgery," part of the humor in this piece is based on the premise that physical pain can be funny. Kistunov, a bank official verbally and physically harassed by a woman seeking money from him, suffers from gout. The pain the woman inflicts on Kistunov might be funny if Kistunov were presented as a figure deserving discomfort—a pompous, stuffy plutocrat, for example. Kistunov is, instead, a rather nervous Casper Milquetoast kind of fellow. The working-class woman, on the other hand, is so obnoxiously aggressive it is impossible to laugh at her "zaniness," and, so, laugh at a reversal in which the "humble" working-class figure runs roughshod over the "lofty" bank official.

The other three sketches are better. "The Drowned Man," unlike "Surgery," is a successful vaudevillian farce. Its basic premise is an inviting one: a convention-bound man, played by the Writer, is approached by a Tramp who asks him to pay to see the Tramp drown himself. The Writer judges the Tramp insane, but the Tramp persistently argues that while the entertainment he is offering is highly unusual, it is an old routine of his; for he intends only to pretend to drown—as he has pretended to do, for money, on many previous occasions. Bewildered by the Tramp's cavalier attitude toward his "show biz" act, the Writer calls a policeman over and tells him the Tramp is deranged. The farce picks up speed when the policeman treats the Tramp's proposition as matter-of-factly as the Tramp does. The policeman advises the Writer to barter for a cheaper entertainment fee. Utterly confused, the Writer finds himself dickering with the Tramp—until the Tramp suddenly agrees to perform for a smaller sum. Only then does the Tramp inform the Writer that he does not know how to swim and depends upon a partner's assistance. He tells the Writer to be sure and shout for "Popnichefsky" to come rescue him. But the addled Writer becomes so fascinated with the Tramp's "realistic" performance he forgets the assistant's name while the Tramp gurgles his last gurgle. The Tramp's hawkerlike patter, the screwball plot, and the Writer's increasing bewilderment create a delightful skit.

The first part of "The Audition" could be based on Simon's own experiences while listening to actors audition. The plot centers on a Girl who has never auditioned before. It would be expected that she do poorly. One interesting plot twist is that the Girl proves more than a little skillful while trying to maneuver herself into a favorable position with her interviewer, the author of the play the Girl is trying out for. Another nice switch is that, although an amateur from the provinces, the Girl has a great deal of natural acting ability. Asked her age, the Girl manages to postpone giving a precise answer until she has wangled the information out of the playwright that the role she is being considered for is the role of a twenty-two-year-old woman. She then announces she is twenty-two. She gains sympathy for herself by letting the interviewer know she is running a temperature; but she smoothly sidesteps the interviewer's advice that she go right home to bed. Still later, when it again appears she is not actually going to get a chance to audition, she feeds the playwright's ego by telling him she has read everything he has written. Nonetheless, she is by no means all guile and bluff. She *is* familiar with the playwright's works, for—finally given her chance—she movingly recites various roles from Chekhov's *Three Sisters*.

The dialogue in the play's final sketch, "The Arrangement," is often vintage Simon. As in "The Drowned Man" and "The Audition," here plot and characterization are deftly interwoven. The plot pivots on a Father's plan to give his son, the Boy, a special birthday gift now that the Boy is on the brink of manhood. The Father intends to arrange and pay for the Boy's first sexual experience, an experience that the terribly shy, immature Boy is in no hurry to have. Although he appears firm of mind, the Father's frugality spurs him to try—ultimately with only a little success—to barter with the Girl, a prostitute, regarding her price. Another key trait in the Father's character is his acute awareness of time passing. His son's bashfulness reminds him of his own bashfulness when *his* father provided him with his initial sexual experience.

The father starts out in full command. He gives his son a last-minute pep talk. A little irritated at his son's naiveté, he asks if the Boy and his friends ever discuss sex. The Boy says, "All the time. But we get too excited to listen" (464). The Father begins to waver in resolution when the Boy's nervousness mounts, rather than declines, during the pep talk. The Boy asks, "Aren't there other ways to become a man? I mean, couldn't I grow a moustache?" (465).

Nevertheless, the Father proceeds to discuss the impending event with the Girl. He begins, "I would like to discuss with you a subject of some delicacy." "Thirty rubles!" the Girl declares. When the Father asks, "Would you consider fifteen rubles?" the Girl replies, "For fifteen rubles I read *Peter Rabbitt* [*sic*]" (467). In a droll turnaround, the Father becomes increasingly awkward in the face of the Girl's salty cocksureness. After reaching financial accord with the Girl, however, the Father informs his son that everything is set. With a sigh, the Boy says, "When I come down those stairs and out into the street . . . I won't be your little Antosha any more . . . I'll be Anton the Man" (469). Suddenly the Father has second thoughts. He is reminded again of the passing of time. Now, too, he is reminded of his own aging and that soon enough his son will become aware that his father only pretends to be a completely confident, resolute man who, therefore, rightfully rules the family. In a charming playlet-ending reversal for which Simon, in this case, did lay the groundwork, the Father quickly convinces his son that this year's birthday present should, after all, be an umbrella. "There's plenty of time next year," the Father states, "to become a man" (470).

The superior quality of most of the material in Act Two, plus the charm of the musical interlude in Act One, plus the humorous insights in the two-part monologue defining a writer—all adds up to a fair number of pluses for *The Good Doctor*. So, too, many of the skits could be staged individually with complete success by acting groups ranging from professional companies to high-school drama clubs. Yet only "The Drowned Man" and "The Arrangement" are first-rate creative efforts; and that is not enough to rank *The Good Doctor* very high up on the hierarchy of Neil Simon's work.

God's Favorite

Simon has had a particularly difficult time being objective about *God's Favorite*. Simon, like almost every other writer, has a natural tendency to see his artistic efforts in the best possible light. But the main reason for his lack of objectivity concerning *God's Favorite* is a personal one. The play represented Simon's first attempt—albeit a very indirect one—to cope with the feelings bred in him by his first wife's death.

The plot of *God's Favorite* is loosely based on the Book of Job. Simon's story starts with someone (who turns out to be named Sidney Lipton) trying to sneak into the living room of Joe Benjamin's palatial home. Lipton flees when the burglar alarm goes off and Joe and two of his offspring, Ben and Sarah, come downstairs. The phone starts ringing. The second phonecall is from a woman inquiring if Lipton is there; the Benjamins know nobody by that name and tell the woman so. Rose, Joe's wife, enters wearing earplugs that prevent her from hearing what is said to her. Joe's third offspring, David, comes home drunk. After the others leave, David tells Joe how much he scorns his father's beliefs. Joe describes his younger years and states his acceptance of his mother's belief, "What God has given, God can take away."[7] He also emphasizes that he gives half the money he makes away to charity. Later, Joe discovers that Lipton has sneaked into the room. A messenger for God, Lipton announces that God is going to test Joe's faith by striking him with misfortune.

Within two weeks, Joe has suffered several financial and domestic setbacks. Lipton returns to tell Joe that worse torments, including bodily pain, will be inflicted on him. He offers Joe the chance to cancel the oncoming suffering by signing a religious renunciation. Joe spurns the offer. In less than a week's time, the house has burned down and Joe is in acute physical pain. When Joe still refuses to renounce God, his wife, Rose, and Ben, Sarah, and the two servants leave him. David, drunk, has already run from the house. Lipton returns to try once more—in vain— to tempt Joe into forsaking his faith. David, now blind, staggers back home. Joe explodes with anger, but still accepts God's will. A bolt of lightning flashes, and David is cured of his blindness. Repentant for having abandoned Joe, all the others return. Joe, physically healthy again, is touched most of all by David's newfound devoutness.

God's Favorite is the poorest play Simon has written. Even the early scenes in *The Prisoner of Second Avenue* have more substance and are far more clever. Despite basing his plot on the Book of Job, Simon neglected to utilize some of the best elements in the biblical story. Unlike Job, Joe neither leads an active religious life day by day nor verbally challenges God's actions. Although Job's wife played only a minor role in the story, it was a powerful role. Torn between her religious beliefs and her love for her suffering husband, she begs Job to end his misery by provoking God to kill him. "Curse God, and die," she pleads. Rose, Joe's wife, plays no significant role whatever in Simon's play. The debate between Job and his comforters is one of the richest sequences in the history of literature. Simon eliminates the comforters from his version of the story.

A worse problem is that what Simon invented to replace the original material is woefully inadequate. Because so little happens in terms of plot development, the play's main emphasis is on its many characters. All the characters surrounding Joe, however, are flimsier creations than he is. Rose has only one characteristic—primitive greed. Ben and Sarah are tediously simpleminded. David's foremost traits, his heavy drinking and relentless cynicism, are never explained. He is so savagely disrespectful to his father it is difficult to understand why he remains the apple of his father's eye. He jeeringly refers to the family's indulging itself in creature comforts, yet he is equally willing to live off of Joe's money. He literally drinks himself blind; but the blindness seems merely a mechanical plot device to enable a miracle to occur so that David can convert to an orthodox religious belief.

Three other characters are brought on stage. Morris and Mandy are black servants who merely crack a few jokes that rely on the audience's knowledge of stereotyped black domestics. For the most part, Lipton is an ineffectual bungler. He could have become a variation of some of the humorously inept "angels" that appeared in films such as *It's a Wonderful Life*. Yet, although he instigates the only mildly interesting conflict in the play, little of Lipton's potential as a character is tapped.

The first scene features the family's reactions to what they believe to be an attempted burglary. The scene is ruined by a plethora of various kinds of repetition. Ben and Sarah numbingly repeat what the other says. This would eventually prove boring even if the original remarks were funny; it becomes instantly boring when, as is almost always the case, the original remarks are trite. Because Rose wears earplugs, every innocuous comment directed to her is repeated ever more loudly, over and over. Even the comparatively less banal exchanges between Joe and David depend on the humor in such dialogue as Joe's saying, "Ohhh, David! David David David David David David David David David David David David David David David David!" and David's response, "Are you talking to me, Dad?" (490–91). There are also running gags. One revolves around Sarah's simultaneous fear of being raped and desire to be raped. When Lipton and Joe talk at the end of the first scene, the repetitions go right on. After several minutes of already slow-moving dialogue, Lipton declares, "All right, enough chitchat, enough fiddle-faddle, enough fencing with each other. Let's get down to brass tacks, Joe Benjamin. Let's discuss the reason of the mysterious midnight visit of this most curious and somewhat sinister figure standing in front of you. Why, at this hour, on this night, in this year, in this city, in this house, on this rug, in these shoes, do I, Sidney Leonard Lipton stand before you? WHAT BUSINESS DO WE, STRANGERS TILL NOT FIVE MINUTES AGO, HAVE UNTO EACH OTHER?" (499). In this snail's pace fashion, it is finally established that God has decided to test Joe. Yet, even then, Lipton laboriously repeats the crux of the plot by insisting on reading the official written version of God's intentions.

The play's structure suffers in other ways. Why Lipton tried to sneak into the house is never clarified; for Lipton told his wife where he would be, and, as he expected, she phoned the Benjamin home to inquire about her husband. More than that, Lipton had been instructed to read God's message to Joe. Obviously, then, he should simply have rung the front doorbell. Joe's initial attempts to protect his home from burglars—his burglar alarm system, his readiness to use force against intruders—are undercut when he suddenly announces to his family that "whatever happens, happens. How we live and how we die is in the hands of our maker" (489). This speech is surprising in another, more fundamental way. Its insistence on Joe's devout religious orthodoxy contrasts with the complete absence earlier in the play of any spiritual awareness on the part of anyone in the family, including Joe. Similarly, Joe's long recapitulation of his early life is unconvincing because it in no way relates to anything that occurs on stage in the daily life of the Benjamins. It is equally hard to accept in realistic terms that Joe gives half of his earnings to charity. If he did, his business could not continue to prosper the way the audience is told it does. Also, his family is too self-indulgent (and, in the mother's case, just plain greedy) to acquiesce to Joe's giving away all that money.

Scene Two concentrates on the family's reactions to the first discomforts caused by the reversal in Joe's fortunes and on Lipton's informing Joe of the worse misfortunes to come. In the previous scene, Joe told Lipton, "I will *not* renounce God. I will *never* renounce God" (508). In Scene Two, he proves true to his word. Joe's religious devotion, however, is simplistic; it is never reinforced by any carefully thought-out creed. Thus, Joe's refusal to forsake his faith seems to result only from his stubborn streak—a trait highlighted when he stolidly opposes some of his family's nagging demands on him. His stubbornness is the only thing that accounts for his otherwise inexplicable intense love for cold-hearted David. This trait also prevents the play from generating excitement, comic or somewhat serious, by means of the misfortune-battered Joe's experiencing an inner conflict concerning his belief in God's goodness.

Only when Joe and Lipton talk privately again does any conflict occur. In Scene One, when Joe declared that he would never renounce God, Lipton remarked, "Renounce, don't renounce, what do I care?" (508). In Scene Two, Lipton suddenly does care—as if Simon happened to spot the chance to liven up the action. Now, Lipton's retaining his "job" depends on his tempting Joe into renouncing God. Joe, stubborn as ever, refuses to do so.

In Act Two, the basic situation in the previous scene is repeated. Joe's misfortunes and sufferings have increased. As Simon did in two playlets in *The Good Doctor,* he tries in *God's Favorite* to make physical pain funny by having Joe, unable to bear being touched, accidentally touched by various members of the family. After Joe's family and servants desert him and then Lipton departs, having failed again to induce Joe to abandon his faith, David returns—blind. Simon makes this the ultimate temptation for Joe. Furious, Joe shouts, "I AM ANGRY AT YOU, GOD! REALLY, REALLY ANGRY!" But he does not elaborate on his feelings in any way. Instead, he immediately proclaims, "And *STILL* I don't renounce you!" (543). And that is the abrupt climax of the play.

It might well be that in *God's Favorite* Simon's attempt to make physical pain funny reflected, in part, his attempt to cope with the pain his first wife endured when stricken with cancer. In any case, it is certainly significant that the climax of *God's Favorite* is Joe's temptation to renounce his faith while having to witness the suffering of someone he dearly loves. It goes a long way toward explaining why Simon wrote the play. Several years after the play opened on Broadway, Simon said that *God's Favorite* was "the play I'm least objective about, because it was written under the most grueling circumstances: It was an attempt to release or exorcise some of the anguish I was going through following the death of my wife. I was not able to rationalize why somebody like Joan could die of cancer at the age of 39. I was very angry, and writing that play was a kind of cathartic experience for me. . . . It was depressing, yet it was something I wanted to do at that point in my life. I was in the middle of the ocean, looking for a log to hang on to, and *God's Favorite* was the log that I grabbed."[8]

California Suite

After experimenting successfully and unsuccessfully in a variety of ways in *The Gingerbread Lady, The Sunshine Boys, The Good Doctor,* and *God's Favorite,* Simon returned to the form he had utilized so skillfully in *Plaza Suite*—a series of original one-act plays. Commenting on why he particularly enjoys this form, he stated that with a one-acter "you can get straight to the big scenes, the crucial moments, the immediate laughs."[9] *California Suite,* composed of four one-act plays taking place in the same suite of a Los Angeles hotel, is a distinct triumph for Simon.

The first playlet, "Visitor from New York," centers on where Jenny, the seventeen-year-old offspring of the now-divorced Bill and Hannah Warren, will spend her senior year in high school. Since the divorce nine years earlier, Hannah, a New Yorker, has had custody of Jenny for all but two summer months out of each year. Now Jenny on her own initiative has flown to California to be with her father and wants to remain with him indefinitely. Hannah waits in the suite in order to meet with her ex-husband. When Bill arrives, they discuss whether Jenny will remain in California or return to New York City with her mother. The final decision is that Jenny will stay in the West.

For a long time during the discussion, it appears there can be but one outcome: Jenny will return to New York. In addition to having a far stronger legal position than Bill, Hannah dominates the conversation. She begins to needle Bill almost immediately. She attacks his manhood by playing on the fact that his West Coast friends call him "Billy" instead of "Bill." She comments, "A forty-five-year-old Billy. Standing there in his cute little sneakers and sweater. Please, sit down, Billy, I'm beginning to feel like your math teacher."[10] She also points out that Jenny's intellectual sharpness has decreased since she resumed living with her father. Hannah lashes out at the California school system and cultural environment.

Yet it gradually dawns on the audience that, despite her intimidating personality, Hannah may not win the battle. She herself is not truly all that confident of victory. Quite early in the conversation, she makes a telling verbal slip. She says, "If I'm going to turn my daughter over to you" (557). Trying to erase her error, she quickly insists that Jenny cannot stay with Bill; but this very insistence reinforces a suspicion that Hannah is not positive she is going to get her way.

Other indications that Hannah is not invulnerable manifest themselves even before she talks with Bill. In the opening playlet of *Plaza Suite,* as a signal of defeat, Simon had room service completely disregard Karen Nash's order not to bring her any anchovies. In *California Suite,* Hannah orders drinks for Bill and herself, but no drinks are ever brought. When Hannah converses with her lover over the phone, she overinsists she is not worried about her problems with Jenny. Before she joins Bill in the other room, she repeatedly checks on her appearance in the mirror; soon after they exchange greetings, she pressures him to compliment her on her looks.

The longer Hannah and Bill converse, the more ground Hannah surrenders. She admits that the New York environment is not a happy

one, although she claims that the turmoil in New York nurtures its
dwellers' creative impulses and prods them into utilizing their potential.
Despite taunting Bill, she acknowledges her admiration for him. When
he punctures her sweeping generalization about how much better East
Coast life is than West Coast life, she blurts out, "Sometimes, I actually
miss you" (563). It also becomes apparent that Bill is not simply a
standing target for Hannah's verbal arrows. He appears more casual,
low-key, and acquiescent than he is. He has had problems with insomnia
and sedatives, and has undergone analysis. He cuttingly satirizes the
culturally and politically "hip" easterners who frequent such places as
Martha's Vineyard. Hitting back directly at Hannah, he informs her,
"You used to be bright and witty. Now you're just snide and sarcastic"
(559).

Then Bill makes a tactical mistake. He becomes too aggressive,
directly threatening to keep Jenny. Instantly Hannah returns to the
attack. She reminds Bill that she can phone her "friend, the Attorney
General of the United States" (564), and get the legal results she wants.
When Bill backs off, however, and resumes employing subtler tactics,
Hannah gives ground even faster than before. Bill asks her how much
time she spends with Jenny, for he knows she feels guilty about spending
most of her time pursuing her professional career. He soon follows this
up by saying, "You know if we leave it up to Jenny, you don't stand a
chance in hell of getting her on that plane. Right?" Hannah can only
reply, "Certainly," adding, "Who said we don't have problems?" (565).
When, goaded by Hannah's verbal jabs, Bill tells her that he does not
like the person she has become, she says, "It's okay. I'm not always fond
of me either" (566). Finally, letting her guard down completely, Hannah
asks, "What are we going to do, Billy? I want my daughter back. You're
the only one who can help me" (566).

What Bill realizes during the course of the conversation is that if he
resists trying to slug it out verbally with Hannah, he will win the battle.
What the equally intelligent Hannah perceives is that she can win
eventually if she resists trying to win *now*. Bill, aware she is softening,
begins to press her for a decision. He declares he will abide by and, more,
support whatever decision Hannah makes. Hannah—no fool—
comments on "what a cunning bastard" (569) he is. She intuits that,
paradoxically, her more powerful position makes her more vulnerable
than Bill's "helpless" position makes him; for as soon as she makes the
decision, she is open to attack. Thus, she agrees to let Jenny stay with
Bill, although on her conditions. She states, "If I have to give her up to

get her back, then let's do it" (570). She agrees, too, because it is painful for her to give Jenny up, and, somewhat the puritan, she feels that if something is painful to do, it is probably the right thing to do.

All this while, Simon subtly indicates that Hannah and Bill are engaged in more than a debate about their daughter. They are also confronting time. Both have had physical setbacks—Hannah, a hysterectomy, Bill, prostate trouble. In response to Bill's accusation that she is now snide and sarcastic, Hannah comments, with more truth than sarcasm, "It comes with age" (599). Both feel the need to do something with their lives now, after having misused so much of their time in the preceding years. After Hannah and he split up, for instance, Bill married again; but he divorced his second wife and is currently living with a divorced actress. Hannah extols the virtues of her lover, yet she goes on to state that he has a heart condition, asthma, and an alcohol problem. She tries to give value to the ambivalent moil of emotions inside her concerning Jenny by stressing that conflict and tension are not only normal, but stimulating.

At another point, by no coincidence, Hannah speaks of her mother. In doing so, she alludes to a deep fear that rendered her even more vulnerable in her present predicament than Bill or Hannah herself realized. Hannah and her mother have never gotten along well. Thus, Hannah is willing to surrender Jenny to Bill for a short while because she fears that if she does not do this, Jenny and she will end up in as loveless a relationship as exists between Hannah and her mother.

Wistfully, Hannah asks Bill what he looks forward to. Unlike Hannah, Bill to some degree has made peace with himself. He tells her he especially enjoys Saturdays. Hannah asks, "Is being in love better now?" Bill says, "Yes." When Hannah asks why, Bill replies, "Because it's now" (568). After predicting to Bill that her lover, given his physical ailments and his life-style, will soon die, Hannah articulates what she hopes to find in her future. She says, "I look forward to a granddaughter . . . I think I screwed up the first time" (566). By this focus on time and aging and on someone who is much less self-assured than would at first appear to be the case, this playlet deals dramatically with what "The Arrangement" in *The Good Doctor* dealt with more lightly.

Both the second and fourth one-acters are examples of broad comedy at its best. In "Visitor from Philadelphia," Marvin, a happily married man who has come to California to attend his nephew's Bar Mitzvah, wakes up in the suite and finds a call girl—out cold—lying next to him. Woozily, he remembers that when he returned to the suite the night before, the girl, sent as a "surprise package" by Marvin's brother, was waiting for him. The only other thing he remembers is that the girl drank more than he did. Because his wife, Millie, is flying into town this morning, Marvin tries fruitlessly to get the girl out of the suite before his wife arrives. When his wife shows up, he continues his increasingly frantic efforts to escape unscathed from his predicament by keeping Millie out of the bedroom. Completely unsuccessful, Marvin has to beg his wife to forgive him for this first—and, he promises, last—infidelity. Millie does forgive him, but vows, as "compensation," to go on a buying spree that will cost Marvin a small fortune.

In "Visitors from Chicago," two couples, the Hollenders and the Franklyns, are on the last leg of a long vacation together. Living in the other couple's company day after day, they have wearied of each other. When Beth Hollender sprains her ankle while all of them are playing tennis, the Hollenders irrationally blame the Franklyns for Beth's accident. This accusation releases the pent-up hostility in all four people. A series of physical accidents, caused by fatigue and emotional upset, ensues—Simon proving here far more able to make physical pain funny than he did in his previous two plays. Each accident triggers more insults. Ultimately the four friends attack each other physically as well as verbally. In the final fight, Mort Hollender incongruously tries to choke Stu Franklyn into declaring he would love the chance to go on another vacation with the Hollenders.

The nearest this last skit comes to having a "message" is when Mort Hollender observes that "four people taking a vacation together can get very testy" because "you can start to get on each other's nerves" (620). Otherwise, this skit is "only" a genuinely zany broad comedy. In "Visitor from Philadelphia," Marvin's attempt to lug the zonked-out call girl into the hallway while his wife sits in the next room constitutes bedroom farce at its finest. The marriage between Marvin and Millie, however, is sketched in enough to make Marvin's confession to Millie of his infidelity both sad and tender. Millie's pain and humiliation are equally moving, especially when her children phone her long distance. As Millie picks up the phone and sits on the bed, the still-asleep call girl turns toward her. With the girl's arm flopping in her lap, Millie must reassure her children that everything is just fine. Simon, once more featuring the subject of the family, dramatizes here a poignant sacrifice a woman makes in order to keep her family intact.

"Visitors from London" is an even finer achievement than "Visitor from New York." Its compelling characters are delineated by means of an absorbing, deftly unfolded plot. As the playlet begins, Sidney Nichols and his wife, Diana, an actress nominated for an Oscar, are dressing to go to the Academy Awards presentation. The only cause for Diana's tenseness and irritability seems to be her concern about whether she will win an Oscar or not. In the second scene, the Nicholses return from the ceremony. Diana did not win an Oscar, and both Sidney and she are drunk. Slowly but relentlessly, the evening's disappointment brings the deep troubles in their marriage to the surface. Sidney is a bisexual, and Diana is unable to dilute the anger, hurt, and fears bred in her by his infidelity. Yet, after finally giving vent to their negative—as well as their positive—feelings about each other, they end the evening by making love.

While dressing, Diana, like Hannah Warren, fusses about her appearance because she is unsure of herself. Diana, too, seeks instant assurance, urging Sidney to compliment her. Her insecurity intensifies when the producer of the picture for which she earned the Awards nomination phones her suite. She does not want to talk with him. When she does, she says that she wants to win the Oscar so that the producer will be rewarded artistically and financially for having starred her in the picture. Her obvious hunger for adulation shows that she wants to win the Oscar for herself; yet, basically unsure of her worth, she does want to please the producer, too.

Diana and Hannah are, however, different in fundamental ways. Diana's insecurity leads her to relish being an actress, relish pretending to be someone else. She feels "much more comfortable as someone else" (594). Hannah, a much stronger personality, always wants to be herself and to conquer, not circumvent, her self-doubts. Diana's happiness vitally depends on the interaction between her and everyone else around her, while Hannah cares about only a few other people's opinions. Hannah's work increases her sense of independence; Diana's work never does so.

Two or three early comments Diana and Sidney make hint that there is tension in this intelligent, witty couple's marriage. For example, Diana, intensely nervous, thinks that her dress bunches up at one shoulder, giving her a "hump." Her concern leads to a flip remark that reveals the tip of an iceberg. Discussing ways to hide her "hump," Diana comments, "If I win, we'll go up together, your arm around me, and they'll think we're still mad for each other after twelve years" (594). Diana and

Sidney are not yet upset or drunk enough, however, to confront their
marital problems. They ask themselves, instead, why they are attending
this nerve-racking Awards ceremony. Sidney flippantly remarks that they have come because "it's all free"
(593). This proves to be an illusion. As the sexually unfaithful Marvin
will learn when his wife goes on her buying spree (and as Chuck Baxter
and Fran Kubelik in *Promises, Promises* learned), the Nicholses learn that
there is always a price to be paid. During their postceremony argument,
in fact, Diana will shout, "I am tired of paying for everything and
getting nothing back in return" (611). In the first scene, Sidney also
states that he "wouldn't miss this circus for the world" (595). But Sidney
is not, as he implies here, merely a bemused spectator at the "circus."
Badgered by Diana, who kept a close eye on him at the party following
the ceremony, Sidney is forced to confess he came to California in order to
make new contacts with homosexuals.

In Scene One, Diana circles back to the theme of payment or chastise-
ment. With tongue in cheek, she informs Sidney that she would have a
much better chance of winning an Oscar if she had sentiment on her side,
something she would surely get if her husband were dying. Then, feeling
a little uneasy, she remarks, "We *are* terrible, Sidney, aren't we? God
will punish us." Sidney replies, with momentary frankness, "I think He
already has" (597). Diana is punished for her egotism when, at the party,
she is forced to watch her husband set up a homosexual rendezvous. Both
of them are, in fact, often unhappy.

In the first scene, Diana specifies one reason she will attend the
ceremony despite the near-panic it fosters in her. She remarks, "I've
always been unhappy. I think that's why I'm such a damned good
actress" (598). Her insistence on the positive value of unhappiness is in
part a pathetic rationalization—but only in part. Like Hannah, Diana
truly believes that unhappiness is the norm, and that happiness is only
lucky happenstance. Both women also link emotional turmoil with
creativity. Later in the evening, Diana declares, "I'm an artist. I'm
creatively unhappy" (609). She implies that because unhappiness breeds
art, one can be either an artist or happy. Her success as an actress results
in no small measure from her unhappiness in private life. Her career
proves she functions successfully as an actress while burdened with
unhappiness. All this goes a long way toward explaining why she has
remained married to a man who causes her such anguish.

Yet at times she disregards her own beliefs. She strives to be both a
successful artist and a happy artist. She also seeks the joy of being

praised, although she expects to have to work hard for such praise. She does not expect Sidney to toss lavish compliments her way, for she knows that he has superior, demanding taste. She admits how much she envies him, explaining, "You have nothing *but* talent. You cook better than I do, you write better than I do, God knows, you *dress* better than I do. . . . And you speak better than I do" (598). Discussing acting talent, she adds, "You had more promise than any of us" (599).

As she continues to praise Sidney, the underlying problem in their marriage is once more faintly alluded to. Diana remarks, "You were so gentle on the stage. So unselfish, so giving." Sensing the drift of her comments, Sidney says, "Yes. I would have made a wonderful Ophelia." Diana responds, "Well, as a matter of fact, you would" (599). Simon's plays usually feature excellent plot situations and vibrant characters. In this playlet, however, he offers more than that. He stresses plot development. The gradual unfolding of the most serious cause of the Nicholses' marital strife—Sidney's bisexuality—is set forth with great skill.

In Scene Two, they return from the bitterly disappointing Awards ceremony and postpresentations party after having consumed a generous amount of alcohol. It is the wee hours of the morning. Drunkenly confused, Diana thinks at first that the room they are in is not theirs; she asks Sidney how long he is going to remain sitting in the wrong suite. But her exact question—"How long do you intend going on like this?"—has deeper implications.

Soon, because she feels particularly rejected on this night, Diana lashes out at Sidney. Her intense uncertainty about everything in her life is pinpointed vividly when she tells Sidney she was aware that, when another actress was announced as the winner of the Academy Award, Sidney's whole body relaxed. She continues, "What could have caused such joy, I wondered to myself. Happy that it was finally over . . . or just happy?" (608). Although stung by her insinuation that he would not want her to win, Sidney answers, "I am sincerely sorry you lost tonight" (609). The sincerity and dignity of his response fail to assuage her misery. She attacks his sexual preferences directly until he finally tells her to go to hell.

All her reserve having already crumbled, Diana maliciously gloats about the breakdown of Sidney's reserve. She says, "What's this? A direct assault? A frontal attack? That's not like you, Sidney" (609). Her satisfaction also underscores how desperately Diana wants some kind of intense emotional response from Sidney. Egotistical, insatiably hungry for attention, she wants a *total* commitment from others. She shouts, "Why don't you love me?" When Sidney replies that he has never stopped loving her "in his way," she says, "Your way doesn't do me any good. I want you to love me in *my* way" (611). Although she knows that sex alone cannot satisfy her, Diana, woefully unsure of herself, longs for the concreteness of a sexual display of love. Hence, when Sidney agrees to make love to her this night, Diana does not want him to close his eyes, for that would allow him, if he wished, to pretend she is someone else.

Their savage confrontation having proved at least temporarily cathartic, Diana and Sidney will remain married, for each helps the other in a variety of ways. One practical advantage of their marriage for Sidney is that by accompanying her everywhere, he makes more sexual contacts than he would be able to do otherwise. Diana acknowledges that Sidney tutors her in taste. Sidney pinpoints less mundane ways in which they aid each other. He states, "We are each a refuge for our disappointments out there" (613). Diana realizes that, whatever Sidney does not provide her with, he does give her his strength and assistance—something that Evy, Toby, Jimmy, and Lou in *The Gingerbread Lady* were sadly unable to give each other. When, exasperated with Diana, Sidney tells her he might deliberately take an overdose of Librium, she quickly and sincerely asks, "What would I do without you?" (610).

Diana knows she is shallow, selfish, and spiritually empty. Her professional work fails to protect her from her weaknesses. Nor does it give her sufficient reassurance that she is of worth. She knows, too, that even though the world at large idolizes her and would condemn Sidney for his homosexuality, nevertheless, Sidney is a finer, more admirable person than she is. Almost destructively aware of her shortcomings, Diana is not at all confident that if other men knew her as well as Sidney does, they would offer her the support he offers. Thus, she is both calmed and deeply moved when, just before they leave for the Awards ceremony, Sidney says, "I wish you everything. I wish you luck, I wish you love, I wish you happiness. You're a gifted and remarkable woman" (600).

In an exchange near the end of the one-acter, they themselves succinctly sum up the reasons—pragmatic, pathetic, and very human—they stay together despite the problems and tensions in their relationship. Diana dryly says, "You *do* take care of me, Sidney, I'll say that." He replies, "You scratch my back, I'll scratch yours" (614).

Earlier in the evening, Diana muses aloud about her nomination for the Academy Award. She says, "This whole thing is so bizarre. Eight years with the National Theatre, two Pinter plays, two Becketts, nine

Shakespeare, three Shaws, and I finally get nominated for a nauseating little comedy" (596). Her stress on the illogicality of human existence in relation to the Awards is comic. But the term she uses to sum up the Awards, "bizarre," describes much else in human experience— including the Nicholses' marriage. Diana's remark further explains why Sidney and she stay married. They can accept their bizarre marriage because they consider it no different from the world around them. The normal state of things is bizarre.

Simon himself has summarized his governing point of view in *California Suite*. Asked to elaborate on why he considered this play to be his most optimistic since *Barefoot in the Park*, Simon said, "I'm trying to write about people who have not necessarily an optimistic view of life but certainly a hopeful one."[11] No one in any of the four one-acters is naive or filled with youthful idealism. Bill and Hannah Warren and Sidney and Diana Nichols, in particular, have had to survive some of life's harsher experiences. Yet, despite their misfortunes and despite their vivid awareness of how grim and bitter life can be, all the characters believe that happiness is possible and that positive hopes for the future are not ridiculous. This makes their "yea-saying" to life—and so, too, Simon's "yea-saying" to life—all the more powerful.

Chapter Nine
Chapter Two

Although *God's Favorite* constituted Simon's initial attempt to cope in his creative work with the death of his first wife, Joan, it was not until he wrote *Chapter Two* that he dealt directly with both Joan's death and his second marriage, to actress Marsha Mason. In *Chapter Two,* George Schneider, a writer, returns home from a trip he took to Europe after the death of his wife, Barbara. George's married brother Leo sees immediately that the trip failed to alleviate George's grief. Leo arranges a few dates for George, but the women prove so unsatisfactory that George becomes convinced he is not ready to resume dating. Leo meets Faye Medwick, a former girlfriend of his, and her friend Jennie Malone at a nightclub and presses George—to no avail—to date Jennie. Faye, like Leo, is having serious marital problems; Jennie, recently divorced, has had such dismal experiences on dates that she, too, is not keen on dating again.

Undaunted, Leo writes Jennie's phone number on the back of a slip of paper containing the number of an elderly lady George is considering employing as a research assistant. Attempting to phone the latter woman, George accidentally dials Jennie's number. Before the confusion is straightened out, George and Jennie have become curious enough about each other to arrange, first, a five-minute meeting and then an evening out together. The two quickly fall in love, but, as they do, George begins to feel guilty about finding happiness with another woman so soon after Barbara's death. Upset when he learns George is thinking of marrying Jennie soon, Leo gives Jennie a graphic description of George's initial grief after Barbara died. Although rocked by what Leo says, Jennie decides to do whatever George wants. Despite last-minute misgivings, George asks Jennie to marry him right away.

Back from their honeymoon, George and Jennie argue because George is pulled in one direction by love and in another by guilt. Meanwhile, Leo and Faye rendezvous in Jenny's apartment. Realizing that Leo merely wants some extramarital sex while she wants much more than that, Faye wavers between remaining faithful to her husband and allowing Leo to take her to bed. When Jennie happens to enter the apartment, Faye promptly ends "the affair." Later, George informs Jennie he is going to Los Angeles for a while in order to think objectively about their situation. Jennie, sensing that the crisis in their relationship has come, tells George that they have nothing to be ashamed of, and that she is glad she has fallen in love with the finest man she has ever met. Although very moved by her speech, George leaves. But almost immediately upon arriving in Los Angeles, he realizes he must live in the present, not dwell on the past. He flies right back to New York and resumes his life with Jennie.

The play's first short scenes cover a lot of ground. The letters of condolence George receives, letters specifying what an exceptionally fine person Barbara was, establish the validity of George's lingering grief over her death. Leo's comments reveal that his marriage with Marilyn is in serious trouble. There is also conflict; Leo tries to pull George past his grief and into a new life. The second scene's presentation of Jennie allows the audience to compare her with George. Although Jennie is depressed about the failure of her marriage and about the ensuing divorce, she is handling her unhappiness more successfully than George is his. Unlike George, she is also quite organized and as determined to push ahead with her life as George is reluctant to do so concerning his. The audience learns, too, that Faye's marriage is in as much trouble as Leo's. By means of another contrast, Scene Three underscores George's inertia. Talking on the phone, George rebuffs the effort of Leona Zorn, a recently divorced acquaintance of his, to arrange a dinner date with him. Unlike Leona, George is not even trying to reenter the social world. Responding to Leo's comments, George admits that he believes he will never find love and marital happiness again. He states, "There are no more Barbaras left in the world. If you meet them *once* in your life, God has been more than good to you."[1]

Jennie thinks there is not one mate of the kind that George thinks there cannot be two of. Thus, the only way George and Jennie could cross paths would be by accident. The sole reason they do not quickly end their initial telephone dialogue is that by the time they have solved the confusion about George's dialing the wrong number, they have become interested in the attractive features—the wit, intelligence, and sensitivity—they have noted in each other. Before they remember their vows not to date, they have already taken a few steps, albeit timid ones, toward each other.

George's proposal that Jennie and he meet for just five minutes certainly does not involve him in much of a commitment. Nonetheless, he *is* taking the initiative. He is also following his healthy instincts—he refuses to think too much about the budding relationship, for he knows (without consciously admitting it) that if he does think about what is happening, he will back out of everything. Jennie, too, lets herself move forward, allowing her curiosity about George to dictate her behavior. When they meet face to face for a few minutes and realize that George's brief-look proposal is not really a very good idea, Jennie is still willing to follow George's lead. This will be a major pattern in their relationship.

As George and Jennie learn more about each other, so does the audience. Prodded by George's questions, Jennie describes her marital years with Gus. He did not possess the hard-to-match goodness Barbara did. Jennie hopes to find the courage to strive for a salubrious male-female relationship despite the dismal failure of her first major effort. Convinced that in the past she settled for too little, she has increased her demands in a man. Finding these demands met in George, she soon becomes much less hesitant about developing their relationship than George does. Thus, during the course of the play, Jennie moves a step beyond the point that Bill and Hannah Warren and Sidney and Diana Nichols reached in *California Suite*. The Warrens and Nicholses merely had hopes for the future; Jennie's hopes actually begin to materialize.

While Jennie's success in finding an admirable man is simplifying her life, George's life is growing enormously complicated. Tense, worried, and guilt-ridden, George suddenly suffers from nausea and shortness of breath during an evening out with Jennie. Afraid that the startled Jennie may have second thoughts about him, he apologizes profusely. Jennie reassures him, "You can't lose me. I know a good thing when I see it" (678). Ironically, her very good-nature ess intensifies George's inner conflict. For, originally, because of his love for his first wife, George did not want to make any emotional commitment to another woman. Now, delighted by Jennie, he wants to commit himself to her completely. Simultaneously, he feels increasingly guilty and fearful. Although not as intensely, Paula McFadden in *The Goodbye Girl* is also afraid of too much happiness. Once, half-kiddingly, half-fearfully, she exclaims, "I hate that goddam 'it's wonderful to be alive' feeling." George fears the love he feels for Jennie, for he fears the pain to which such love renders one vulnerable. He fears that his happiness with Jennie will be cruelly snatched away from him. His fear is certainly understandable. He had been supremely happy with Barbara, and suddenly she had died, leaving him in misery. If he becomes supremely happy with Jennie, what assurance does he have that misfortune will not come crashing down on him again? He is acutely aware of life's uncertainties. This also explains why he fears he will lose Jennie through his own blunders.

George's guilt feelings stem in part from his persistent belief that he should not be so happy so soon after his first wife's death. He is flummoxed by having found someone as wonderful as Barbara was after stoutly declaring that he could never meet anyone as wonderful as her. He doggedly insists that "it's not supposed to happen twice in your life" (678). His tendency toward self-pity encourages him to believe he should grieve for Barbara for the rest of his life. He feels, too, that being happy is being disloyal to Barbara. Consequently, he is confused and filled with guilt when he forgets Barbara while he is out with Jennie. Pulled two ways, he says, "I know I'll never stop loving Barbara, but I feel so good about you . . . and I can't get the two things together in my mind" (678).

Jennie says the right thing—namely, that she wants George to have room for all his feelings. She is, however, foolishly optimistic. She thinks she can carry George on her shoulders. She says, "I'm very strong, George. . . . I have enough for both of us. Use it, George" (678). She is strong; but she still only barely prevails, and she makes her task tougher by underestimating the depth of the turmoil in George. Attracted to George's best qualities, Jennie fails to perceive that although George meets her standards, he has fierce problems that will bring her much pain and almost fatally ruin the love between them.

Leo's personal preferences determine his view of the rapidly blooming romance between his brother and Jennie. Not all that interested himself in deep emotional commitments, he does an abrupt about-face concerning George. He stops encouraging George to move forward with his life. Now he advises George to slow down. This is sound advice. For, despite admitting next to nothing to Leo, George is riddled with misgivings. One time, for example, he suddenly phones Jennie to suggest they wait at least a couple of months more before marrying. Leo, in his desire to see the pace slowed down, does not confine his efforts to George. He meets privately with Jennie in order to try to make her less starry-eyed about what she is getting into. He describes in vivid detail George's grief right after Barbara's death, for he believes George needs still more time to cope with that grief before committing himself emotionally to another woman. He explains to Jennie, "I wouldn't want you and George to be hurt because that time was denied to him—to both of you" (696).

Leo's warning is a wise one, and Jennie *is* jarred—for the moment. Yet, although uneasy, she reverts to her earlier optimism. She admits that perhaps she has not "asked enough questions." But then she adds, "I can only deal with one thing at a time. Let me experience my happiness before I start dealing with the tragedies." She clutches at the fact that George's instincts are healthy ones. Reminding Leo that the plan for an immediate marriage was George's plan, she comments, "He picked the date. And if that's not the sign of a man who wants to get healthy quickly, I don't know what is" (699).

Jennie's perceptions about George's instincts for life are right on target. George, nurtured by his life-seeking instincts, will finally choose Jennie and the present over all else. Nonetheless, she is naive. She still greatly underestimates the amount of pain and destruction that will dominate her life with George while he struggles to overcome his obsession with the past. So, too, Jennie's continued reliance on her own strength is glib. She says, "I promise you, Leo, even if what we're doing is not right, I'll *make* it right" (700). Her strength will indeed go far toward carrying the day, but it cannot do the whole job. As she ultimately comprehends, George must use his strength. Before he does so, Jenny finds herself, concerning their relationship, hanging on by her fingernails. In sum, the love between George and Jennie would never have thrived if they paused to reflect carefully before they acted; yet the longer they postpone confronting the central problems existing in their relationship, the more inevitable it becomes that those problems will wreak havoc in their lives.

By the time they return to George's apartment after the honeymoon, George is—as he later puts it—thoroughly "stuck" (729). Still trying to avoid confronting his conflicting thoughts and feelings, he suggests to Jennie they just go to bed. Jennie, however, decides to contend with George's moodiness. This marks a very important change in Jennie's behavior. Previously, she was always willing to follow George's lead. Now, beginning to perceive fully the severity of the danger their relationship is in, she takes the initiative. She will do so even more forcefully on the day George prepares to leave for Los Angeles. On this earlier night, Jennie and George will, in fact, take turns pressing each other to get everything out into the open. Although upset at himself, George is well aware how ready he is to hit out at Jennie. He says, "There are a lot of things I would like to say that would just get us both in trouble. I don't want to deal with it now" (709). Jennie pressures him to speak out, but when he starts talking about both his honeymoon with

Barbara and his honeymoon with Jennie, Jennie backs off. She says, "I think we ought to limit this conversation to present honeymoons. . . . Because that's where we're living." George rightly replies, "You can't get to the present without going through the past" (710)—although he says nothing about his coming to this realization a bit tardily.

Now George criticizes Jennie for not previously asking him more questions about his past. When they do begin asking each other for details about Barbara and Gus, they become increasingly distraught. Realizing that their talk is even more painful for George than for herself, Jennie asks, "Do you think that I'm expecting you to behave a certain way?" This leads George finally to articulate more directly what is gnawing at him. He confesses, "No. *I* expect it. I expect a full commitment from myself. . . . I did it twelve years ago. . . . But I can't do it now" (713). Having revealed this much about his turmoil, George almost immediately deliberately goads Jennie to anger. He pauses in his attack only when Jennie stops bending over backwards to be understanding and, instead, retorts in kind. Obviously Barbara had a temper, and George has come to respect a woman only if she will fight back. Jennie shouts, "You want me to stand toe to toe with you like Barbara did?" With consummate wisdom, Jennie refuses to become Barbara in order to ease George's dilemma of being pulled in two directions by two different women. She states, "I'm not Barbara. And I'll be damned if I'm going to re-create *her* life, just to make *my* life work with you" (713).

Jennie is paying the full price for her earlier shallow optimism and willingness to postpone confrontations. Losing all self-control, George lashes out still more cruelly, even insinuating that Jennie is not as good a person as Barbara was. He continues, "I resent everything you want out of marriage that I've already had. And for making me reach so deep inside to give it to you again. . . . And most of all, I resent not being able to say in front of you . . . that I miss Barbara so much" (714).

Two days later, George decides to go to Los Angeles. This decision infuriates Jennie, for she understands better than ever now that they cannot escape their problems. She attacks George verbally and even physically. She tells him that he makes her furious because he will not "make the slightest effort to opt for happiness" (727). She describes her own emotional turmoil, declaring that, in spite of her anger, she still loves him, and that this love is the most important thing in her life. She knows, too, that his needling of her is, in part, his twisted, frightened way of testing her willingness to stay with him; he has to keep proving to himself that she will not leave him, which he so desperately fears she will. Still, she bluntly informs him that she cannot promise to continue to submit to his tests. She also informs him that she wants everything life has to offer her, a home, a family, a career. She says, "There's no harm in wanting it, George, because there's not a chance in hell we're going to get it all, anyway. But if you don't *want* it, you've got even less chance than that" (728). She believes that George's fear of aiming high and of happiness is wrong; and she insists that George grapple with, not try to evade the tangle of, their marital problems.

Although riveted by what Jennie says, filled with admiration for her, and aware of the validity of her views, George still has not become completely "unstuck." Everything continues to happen too quickly. Significantly, George finally begins to become unstuck only when he thinks of what he used to do when Barbara and he reached an angry impasse. This does not mean that the memory of Barbara has a stranglehold on him. It means that he can think of both Barbara and Jennie and not feel he should exclude one or the other. Equally significant, it also means he can use the past to aid him in the present. For George, the past no longer solely undercuts, negates the present.

Simon in past works stressed the positive aspects of guilt. Feeling guilty meant that a conscience was at work, and this was a good thing. Barney Cashman, for instance, in *Last of the Red-Hot Lovers* feels guilty about his plans to be unfaithful to his wife, and his uneasiness helps him do the right thing in the end. George, on the other hand, learns that his feeling guilty about being happy with Jennie is foolish. In this case, Simon separates guilt feelings and moral uprightness. George's love for Jennie is morally right. His feelings of guilt are destructively repressive—wrong.

In the midst of telling Jennie he has fought his way past his fears and guilt, George announces that he finished the last chapter of his new book. The completion of the book points to another truth George has finally accepted: life consists not of one beginning and ending, but of many beginnings and endings.

Simon's employment of a subplot featuring George's brother Leo and Faye Medwick has been judged "misguided" and "calamitous," wrecking the main plot because it has no relation to it.[2] Actually the subplot offers some vivid similarities to the story of George and Jennie and some vivid contrasts. During her "affair" with Leo, Faye learns the same thing George and Jennie learned when they returned from their honeymoon—namely, that serious marital problems must be confronted. As the play ends, Faye's husband, Sidney, and Faye, at her instigation, are embarking on a confrontation which will arouse as much anger as Jennie and George's confrontation ignited, but which may also make the Medwicks' marriage better.

Leo, on the other hand, never learns anything. His marriage is in a dismal state. Hungry to "make it" financially, he gives his business activities so much preference he is rarely home. He is a poor husband and a poor father. Although his wife, Marilyn, is too inflexible, Leo is the main cause of their marriage's deterioration. He is selfish, immature, and too preoccupied with sex. He condemns Marilyn for not engaging in sexual "craziness" (682); simultaneously, he wants his marriage to revive, somehow, that "feeling you had just before you got married" (682). George realizes it is wrong to stagnate in the past, while Leo never maturely accepts the fact that one cannot return to what is long past.

Faye's marriage is in equally dire straits. Sexual activity has dwindled to almost nothing. Faye, however, is also very interested in nonsexual physical affection. She speaks of feeling envious and depressed when Sidney and she were out with another long-married couple who, as opposed to Sidney and Faye, kept touching each other fondly. Jennie advises Faye to speak to Sidney about their marital woes, but Faye is not yet ready to do that. Like George and Jennie, she postpones thinking clearly about how to try to solve her problems. She decides, instead, to have an affair with Leo. All such an affair means to Leo is a quick coupling in bed; but a "quickie" is not something Faye can blithely participate in. Nor is it what she really wants. (In this sense, Faye is like Barney Cashman in *Last of the Red-Hot Lovers* when he meets Elaine Navazio; and Elaine is like Leo.) When Faye's first rendezvous with Leo falls through, her instincts tell her to end the affair right away. Unfortunately, unlike George and Jennie, she does not obey those good instincts.

When Leo and Faye finally do begin to make love, the phone rings. Leo gave out the phone number because, as always, he puts business first. Thus, the same materialistic drive in Leo that is ruining his marriage now helps to ruin his affair with Faye. For the telephone interruption does for Faye what the honeymoon did for George and Jennie: it gives her time to think. She fully recognizes that for Leo their affair is nothing very special. More importantly, she realizes that she does want something special from a male-female relationship. Although she, too, wants sex, she also wants what Leo is not the least bit interested in; she wants the nonsexual fondling that the long-married couple she observed were engaged in. Most of all, she wants both the sex and the fondling to be kindled by love.

Sparked by Leo's comment that maybe this particular day is not the right time for her, Faye exclaims, "I already tried Transcendental Meditation, health foods and jogging. And I am now serenely, tranquilly and more robustly unhappy than I have ever been before. . . . So don't tell me this isn't the right time, Sidney!" (718–19). Simon overuses the device of a slip of the tongue, a device he relied upon starting with his first play, *Come Blow Your Horn*. Nonetheless, Faye's slip in using her husband's name is in character. It makes her consciously aware that there is only one important man in her life, and it is not Leo. Sidney is the man with whom she wants—and will try again to gain—both sex and romance. Leo, in fact, perceptively sums up the difference between Faye and himself when he says that Faye is a "romantic unhappy woman" and that he is a sexually "frustrated man" (721). Thus, while George is struggling not to feel guilty about falling in love again, Faye envies the love George and Jennie feel. Faye tells Leo, "What I want, I can't have. I want what Jennie has: the excitement of being in love again" (719).

"Want" is the key word. Most of the time, Leo gains what he wants. What he wants, however, is minuscule. Unable to feel again the love he experienced just before his wedding, all Leo seeks now is sex. Jennie, by contrast, gains only a portion of what she wants. Yet, because—as she informed George—she wants everything, her mere partial success brings her much more of life's riches than Leo's near-total success brings him. Although envious of Jennie, Faye accepts—rather than sulks about—being unable to recapture the first lyrical feeling of love. What she does want now and will seek to share with Sidney is a second blossoming of love. Leo wrongheadedly declares, "I have no intention of changing" (731). Faye, like George and Jennie, is trying to change.

Chapter Two is one of Simon's finest achievements. It contains an abundance of high-quality funny lines and several gripping monologues. Through the dialogue and speeches, Simon succeeds once again in combining the comic and the poignant. Moreover, he presents four totally lifelike, totally interesting characters. George, Jennie, Leo, and Faye vibrantly deal with such basic elements of the human experience as happiness and anguish, yearning and acceptance, sex and romance, morality and guilt, and, most of all, love and death. And they do so in confrontations that are sometimes humorous, sometimes taut and painful. In earlier plays such confrontations did not always lead to something better. Oscar and Felix in *The Odd Couple* learn nothing from having it out with each other. The showdown between Karen and Sam Nash in *Plaza Suite* may have only hastened the end of their marriage. But, as was true for Diana and Sidney Nichols in *California Suite,* Jennie and George create a stronger, richer marriage because of the truths they confronted.

Simon does, then, provide a happy ending for *Chapter Two.* But this happy ending, like the ones in *California Suite, The Sunshine Boys,* and *The Prisoner of Second Avenue,* is quite different from the happy endings in Simon's first plays. The family problems in *Come Blow Your Horn* and *Barefoot in the Park* were never really very threatening; they were solved without much pain, and gave way to a rosy future for all. Jennie and George, on the other hand, have to struggle desperately to bring about a happy ending. So, too, whatever happiness they attain in days to come will be tempered by a world that does not devote itself to promoting happiness for human beings and by all the emotional and psychological scars Jennie and George possess as a result of their struggle to gain a valid hope for happiness.

Chapter Ten
Movie Adaptations and Movie Originals

Four Screenplays

Because of Simon's desire to reach a bigger audience than the theater provides, and because his second wife, Marsha Mason, was more involved in screen roles than in stage appearances, Simon gradually became more interested in writing for the movies. This interest intensified when he began working with Hollywood producer Ray Stark and director Herbert Ross, two professionals Simon greatly admired. Yet the quality of the new motion pictures Simon helped create remained as uneven as the quality of the earlier ones. Simon's next two adaptations of his plays serve as a case in point.

The Prisoner of Second Avenue is only moderately successful. The scene presenting Mel and Edna's initial response to the burglarization of their apartment is superb comedy. Soon afterwards, when Edna ceases being merely bewildered all the time by Mel's moods and becomes a more aggressive personality, the movie's energy perks up. A new sequence centered on Edna's appropriation of a wallet from a fellow city-dweller is very funny. But many portions of the film are quite weak. The first long segments, stressing Mel's kvetching about New York City, are repetitious and tedious. The segment featuring Mel's sisters and brother Harry fizzles out quickly. Harry draws attention away from Mel, just as he does in the play, yet in the film version Harry is not as interesting a character as he is in the play. The final scene of the movie seems not as much zany as strained and implausible.

The Sunshine Boys, on the other hand, is one of the best films Simon has scripted. The movie earned Simon some of his most favorable reviews to date. The legendary George Burns won an Oscar for his performance as Al Lewis. This was the first film written by Simon that Herbert Ross directed. Simon later commented, "In a movie, the constant cuts and different camera angles change the rhythm of one's writing. The reason I work best with Herb Ross directing my films is that he understands the rhythm of my writing and tries very hard to keep it."[1] Judith Crist, noting Simon's increased skill as a screenwriter, observed, "Simon's screenplay has 'opened' the play to enriching effect."[2] Not the least important reason for the comparative success of *The Sunshine Boys,* however, is that it has better basic material than *The Prisoner of Second Avenue.*

Herbert Ross had no hand in either *Murder by Death* or *The Cheap Detective. Murder by Death,* an original screenplay, is poor fare. The plot vaguely resembles Agatha Christie's *Ten Little Indians.* A group of people is assembled without initially knowing exactly why they have been brought together. In Simon's version, Lionel Twain, a rich man who fancies himself a peerless, albeit amateur criminologist, is responsible for luring the guests to his mansion and then coercing them to remain there. The guests consist of six famous sleuths, Dick and Dora Charleston (based on Nick and Nora Charles), Sam Diamond (Sam Spade), Sidney Wang (Charlie Chan), Jessica Marbles (Jane Marple), and Milo Perrier (Hercule Poirot), plus their traveling companions. The sleuths undergo various difficulties while journeying to their destination. Once assembled at the dinner table, they are informed by their host that murder will be committed and will prove too much of a puzzle for them to solve. The rest of the plot involves murders actual or fake. Bensonmum, Twain's apparently blind butler, is a central part of the action, and a supposedly deaf-and-dumb maid proves much less inconsequential than she is first believed to be.

The initial premise is clever enough. The first appearances of the Charlestons and the others allow Simon to create some good fun by spoofing the traits of the fictional characters of whom Simon's sleuths are parodies. Simon, however, does not develop his characters any further. In order for the film to succeed, then, it must have a good plot. Unfortunately, the plot is mediocre—belabored, contrived, and unconvincing. In fact, Simon, rarely an outstanding contriver of plots, painted himself into a bad corner. In *Ten Little Indians,* the mystery deepens as one after another of the main characters is killed (or apparently killed). Because Simon wanted all the guests in *Murder by Death* to stay alive so that they could continue to wrestle with the mystery, the murders that occur remain peripheral. Thus, little suspense or tension is generated. So, too, the need to keep track of five sets of major characters necessitated a constant jumping back and forth from one set to another. This drastically undercuts the movie's comic impetus. A final flaw is that the parodies are not funny enough to make the audience forget that the plot is moving along at a snail's pace.

The Cheap Detective echoes the plots in The Maltese Falcon, The Big Sleep, Casablanca, and To Have and Have Not. For example, the film's main character, private detective Lou Peckinpaugh, hunts for the murderer of his partner and for a valuable work of art, while also trying to help the French husband of Marlene DuChard, with whom Lou once had a love affair. This film has faults as serious as those that spoil Murder by Death. In fact, one flaw of the first film is repeated here. Simon again relies too heavily for laughs on the audience's knowledge of the material that his movie spoofs. The Cheap Detective also keeps shuttling back and forth in its references to one Bogart film or another, diluting the overly complicated story's momentum. Perhaps the biggest flaw in the film, however, is Simon's caricature of Humphrey Bogart. Simon limits Lou Peckinpaugh, a role enacted by Peter Falk, to only a few of Bogart's most obvious and superficial characteristics. Lou remains poker-faced almost continuously; and he speaks in a monotone that becomes deadeningly dull.

Yet this film does offer more rewards than Murder by Death. A few characters and scenes are quite entertaining. The widow of Lou's partner, Georgia Merkle, played by Marsha Mason, is breathless, bright-eyed, and outrageously brazen—a femme fatale without a thought in her head about the evil she commits. Concerning Marlene DuChard, Molly Haskell aptly commented that "the best and most original stroke of parody is Louise Fletcher's demystification of the hitherto sacrosanct Ingrid Bergman heroine of Casablanca as a woman whom one character . . . describes as 'the most beautiful, brave, and boring woman I have ever met.' "[3] Parodying The Big Sleep, the best sequence in Simon's film presents Lou's interview with Ann-Margret as the East European vamp Jezebel Dezire and Sid Caesar as her invalid husband.

If the level of entertainment reached in the Dezire sequence had been matched in the movie's other main segments, The Cheap Detective would have been a first-class comedy. Instead, the best that can be said about the picture is that, in comparison with other original screenplays by Simon, it is better than The Out-of-Towners and Murder by Death, but not nearly as good as The Heartbreak Kid or The Goodbye Girl.

The Goodbye Girl

The Goodbye Girl originated by accident. Simon had written another original script titled Bogart Slept Here, the story of what a sudden phenomenal success does to an actor. Robert DeNiro and Marsha Mason were to star in the film, with Mike Nichols directing. Within a week after filming began, it became clear that DeNiro and Nichols were not going to be able to work together successfully. While Nichols and DeNiro went on to other projects, Simon arranged for Richard Dreyfuss to read aloud from the script with Ms. Mason. Intrigued by the artistic rapport that developed between the two performers, Simon decided to write a new story about an actor who is still struggling to make a successful career for himself.

The story opens with Paula McFadden and Lucy, her preteenage daughter, returning to their apartment only to discover that Tony, the man Paula had been living with, has abandoned them, just as Lucy's father did years earlier. That night, Elliot Garfield arrives from Chicago to pursue his acting career in a production of *Richard III*. He expects to find Paula's apartment ready for him to occupy because Tony, without telling Paula, sublet it to Elliot. Elliot offers Paula a compromise: he is willing to share the apartment with Paula and Lucy. Paula, broke and jobless, instantly agrees to his proposal.

When Elliot attends the first rehearsal of *Richard III,* he receives his second major setback. The director has come up with the preposterous idea of portraying Richard as a homosexual. Paula, meanwhile, resumes trying to make a career for herself as a dancer, but with no success. Paula and Elliot meet near the apartment, and, after Elliot persuades Paula to wait for him outside a store, Paula has her purse snatched and blames her misfortunes on Elliot. Nonetheless, Elliot succeeds in gaining Lucy's affections, although he is startled when she declares she does not find him sexy. He also helps Paula out financially until she lands a job.

Paula and Lucy attend the opening night of *Richard III.* As Elliot feared, the production is a fiasco. Later, he impresses Paula when he recites speeches from the play as he wished he could have been allowed to do onstage. Elliot and Paula begin to enjoy each other's company more and more; when Elliot gains employment in an improvisational group, he arranges a rooftop "dinner party" for Paula and himself. Now Paula and Lucy fear that Elliot, like Lucy's father and Tony, will abandon them. Their fears seem confirmed when they learn that Elliot has been given a role in a new film and must fly west immediately. Then Elliot arranges for Paula to travel with him; and she, joyously realizing he really does intend to live with Lucy and herself, tells him to head west on his own.

Simon's film-script hearkens back to the romantic comedies filmed in the late 1930s and the 1940s. Several characters and scenes, especially the lovers' rooftop interlude, evoke memories of earlier film comedies. So does the oddball way Paula and Elliot first meet. Yet the film is often able to have its cake and to eat it, too, for much of the dialogue, many scenes, and several facets of the main characters' personalities are all thoroughly contemporary. The lovers in a 1939 comedy, for instance, would not go to bed together without first getting married. The heroine would not have already been married, given birth to a daughter, and gotten divorced; nor would she have had Paula's other sexual experiences. The dialogue would have been much less sexually explicit. Finally, Elliot would never have played a homosexual Richard III.

Still, the picture's overriding strength is its romantic-comedy mood, which sustains the film even when some of the individual sequences fail to provide much comedy or much romance. The mood is firmly established in the first major sequence, perhaps the best portion of the whole film. This sequence, featuring the maneuvering done by both Paula and Elliot in order to gain living quarters, is fast-paced and funny. There are numerous clever quips. Furthermore, these lines build from a fundamentally humorous central situation. There is also the unflagging and riveting energy possessed by both Elliot and Paula. Indeed, their energy creates a second kind of momentum that reinforces the film's prevailing romantic-comedy mood.

A surprise turn near the end of the first sequence sets up a major part of the rest of the story. Just when Paula seems to have completely triumphed over Elliot by maneuvering him into letting her stay in the apartment, the audience learns that Elliot, although kind-hearted, is no pushover. Promptly following up her initial victory, Paula lists all the rules and regulations she expects Elliot to obey. Finishing her recitation, she asks Elliot if he has everything straight. She is quite taken aback when he says no. She is even more taken aback when he proceeds to rattle off an equally long list of rules and regulations that he expects her to honor. Elliot's counterattack indicates that while the previous men in Paula's life remained passive—until they sneaked away—Elliot will never feel the need to run away from Paula because she threatens to dominate his life. On many occasions, she will not only fail to dominate him, but will have her hands full trying just to hold her own. Later, Elliot will figure out that Paula is used to being the only aggressive partner in a relationship and, therefore, does not know how to live with a man who is not intimidated by her. Ultimately, Paula learns how to take as well as to give in a male-female relationship. She will also admit that, with regard to energy, intelligence, and willpower, she has met her match. At one point, she confesses that Elliot simply wears her out.

Interspersed between their quarrels and good times together, Paula and Elliot have important encounters on their own. Paula's attempt to impress the theater producers at a musical comedy audition is a funny take-off of those movies in which the heroine dramatically steps out of the chorus line into a starring role bringing fame and fortune. Paula, over thirty years old and no longer in tiptop physical condition, huffs and puffs and quips her way through the audition—and does not even get a job in the chorus. Elliot's experiences at the rehearsals of *Richard III* are even better. The funniest single moment in the film occurs when the play director first explains to the cast that he has decided to present a homosexual interpretation of Richard. The gradual registering on Elliot's face of what the director is saying, followed by Elliot's expressions of amazement, disbelief, and incipient agony as he searches the faces of the other actors trying to ascertain if they, too, think that the director is nutty as a fruitcake—all of this builds hilariously.

A later rehearsal scene, in which the director talks the almost panic-stricken Elliot into "trusting" him, is equally good. It also enriches the delineation of Elliot's character by dramatizing that Elliot, like Paula, is not always 100 percent in control of all situations. He, too, suffers defeat. Elliot is, in fact, not as all-confident as he first appears to be. Just as Paula needs to be reassured that she is not going to be abandoned again, Elliot needs to be reassured he is talented and attractive. He is rattled by others' hostility or indifference toward him. His desire that Lucy like him is motivated not only by his genuine fondness for her, but because he wants everyone—even the ten- or eleven-year-olds he meets—to like him.

Although Paula suffers embarrassment during her chorus-line audition, Elliot is later humiliated far more cruelly. He is trapped into giving a ludicrous performance in the godawful opening-night presentation of *Richard III*. (Even the director's mother is reluctant to praise the show.) Yet his defeats strengthen him; he becomes more self-confident than he was when he arrived from Chicago. He shows his increased strength of character by bouncing back from the disaster of *Richard III*. For Paula, he recites passages from the play quite movingly. He quickly finds other employment. When the new job fails to pan out, he joins an improvisational group of actors and does so well he is hired for a choice part in a forthcoming movie.

The Goodbye Girl does have its flaws, however. The bickering between Elliot and Paula in the first half of the film becomes tedious. Paula whines and complains too much, and becomes weepy too often. Her blaming Elliot for her misfortunes after her purse is snatched is silly—it appears to be simply a weak contrivance on Simon's part to keep the romantic conflict going. Although Lucy delivers several funny lines, she is little more than the tough-but-soft, wise-but-innocent, stereotyped youngster seen in many movies.

Yet Lucy is not a detriment to the film because she evokes the aura of romantic comedies. On the contrary, she reinforces precisely the semisentimental upbeat mood that Simon wanted in the movie. In fact, providing his own apt summation of what his script aimed—successfully—to do, Simon said that *The Goodbye Girl* "was an answer to what I felt was happening in the film industry—that there was too much movie violence for the sake of violence. I wanted to write about two people who care for each other and who can show that there's still some love left in the world."[4]

The love that Paula and Elliot come to feel for each other is a love they have to earn. It is not a case of love at first sight. They first have to mature as individuals, mature through painful trials and tribulations and through an increased self-awareness of their faults and weaknesses. Only then can they offer each other a love well worth prizing.

Two More Adaptations

Because the play is poignant, funny, and insightful, the transference of *Chapter Two* to the screen should have produced another superior film based on a Simon script. Instead, the film version is one of the poorest movies Simon has ever participated in creating. The quality of the acting in the film makes it impossible to reevaluate the characters and the basic plot first presented on stage. The only performance that could be described as at least competent is Marsha Mason's. The character of Jennie Malone was based in part on Mason's personality. Mason returned the compliment by projecting facets of that character—such as her vivacity, good-naturedness, and warmth—in her screen performance. Yet even she had acting problems. She is not as convincingly light-hearted and clever in the early scenes as Jennie is supposed to be. She fails to make good use of some of her best lines. Physical mannerisms, such as her habit of pressing the palm of her hand against her chest or forehead, become dullingly repetitious.

The other three major performances range from poor to very poor. Joe Bologna, as Leo Schneider, seems perpetually ill-at-ease. Describing George's breakdown after Barbara's death, Bologna, speaking in a monotonous tone of voice and at breakneck speed, dilutes almost all the power in the speech. Like Marsha Mason, Valerie Harper, as Faye Medwick, fumbles some of her best lines; others are phrased in a manner that renders them incomprehensible. Worst of all, Harper looks so emaciated it is impossible to believe that the character she portrays would be sexually attractive to any man, never mind a lady-killer such as Leo. The worst performance is turned in by James Caan. He mumbles almost all of his part of the banter in the early scenes. His serious lines sound maudlin or lugubrious. He never succeeds in conveying George's grief or intense inner turmoil.

If Simon, producer Ray Stark, and director Robert Moore approved of the actors' performances, they deserve a full share of the blame for the film's dismal quality. Simon must also be criticized for a major blunder in his film adaptation. In order to provide "a bridge" for the scenes in the play that go from the day George and Jennie marry to the evening they return from their honeymoon, Simon added episodes that take place during the honeymoon. The key scene, which is supposed to account for the abrupt swing in George's mood from joyous to morose, occurs on the dance floor. George and Jennie meet a couple who have known George for years. Despite George's explicitly introducing Jennie to the couple as his wife, the couple proceed—at length—to lament the death of Barbara and to praise her highly. It is inconceivable that any two people in their right minds would be guilty of such grossly insensitive behavior. George's willingness to listen to all the couple have to say—instead of telling them to shut up—is contemptible. It would have been better if Simon had written no "bridge" sequence at all.

California Suite, released before *Chapter Two,* is the far better film. It is, for several reasons, also more successful than the film version of *Plaza Suite,* which, as a play, used the same basic format as *California Suite.* The mistake in *Plaza Suite* of having one actor appear in more than one of the stories is not repeated. The pace in *California Suite* is faster because the four stories take place concurrently. Also, the stories are opened up more—occurring in many different localities. Finally, Herbert Ross, the director, saw to it that the acting was uniformly superior in quality.

This is not to say that *California Suite* is flawless. The crosscutting among four plots hurts the two broad comedies. Chopped into several sequences, long and short, these two plots accumulate little comic drive. The skit featuring the two couples on an overlong vacation together is the most fragmented and soon loses whatever original humorous impetus it had. It becomes, in its last segments, too frenetic and strained. A last short scene added to the story of Hannah and Bill Warren, a scene in which Hannah's daughter comes to the airport to tell Hannah goodbye, operates in opposition to the movie's overall time scheme. Hannah rushes off to catch a plane in the late afternoon of the same day that the Nichols set off for the Academy Awards ceremony and that Marvin Michaels returns to his suite to find a call girl waiting for him. Yet Hannah is still at the airport the next day when characters from the other stories arrive to board their planes and when her daughter rushes up to her.

But, enhanced by the superior acting skills of Alan Alda and, especially, Jane Fonda, the earlier scenes between Hannah and Bill are fine. They are increasingly touching. The use of close-ups skillfully conveys the subtle and very significant shifts in mood that Hannah experiences. The sadness of the Warrens' lives becomes quite moving. Still, the best story in the play, that of Diana and Sidney Nichols, is the best story in the movie. The couple's stiff-upper-lip wit comes across winningly, with great charm and style. The anger fanned by the evening's bitter disappointment and by the large amount of alcohol the Nicholses consume rises to the surface in a thoroughly compelling fashion. Yet the anger never overwhelms this couple's intelligence or their capacity for tenderness. The script is also helped by the superb performances of Michael Caine and Maggie Smith, who won an Academy Award for Best Supporting Actress for 1978.

Thus, even in these later years when Simon's interest in film had intensified, the quality of his work for the cinema continued to ride a seesaw.

Chapter Eleven
Later Efforts
They're Playing Our Song

Although Simon has stated that he is not particularly fond of writing Broadway musicals, he continues to return periodically to the musical-comedy genre. One such time occurred when he became intrigued by the basic plot possibilities of *They're Playing Our Song,* for which Marvin Hamlisch wrote the melodies and Carole Bayer Sager the lyrics.

The story begins with the first meeting of its two characters, Vernon Gersch, a songwriter, and Sonia Walsk, a lyricist. Vernon has won an Oscar, among other awards, while Sonia has had only one big hit to her credit. Soon after the two start working together, Sonia suggests that the quality of their songs could be improved if they knew each other a little better. They go to a nightclub and, later, spend a weekend together. Sonia, however, is still entangled with Leon, an ex-boyfriend who, even after she moves into Vernon's apartment, continues to press her for attention. Vernon also feels intimidated by Sonia's forceful personality. Finally, because Vernon becomes uncertain whether he wants solely a professional relationship with Sonia or solely a personal relationship or both, the two go their separate ways. Then, discovering how much they love each other, they ultimately choose to live together permanently.

The play has several weaknesses. Vernon is as thin a character as those in *God's Favorite.* He speaks frequently of his various idiosyncracies, but on stage he does little except deliver quips. The flimsiness of the material led Simon to employ what he often resorts to when he needs to pad his plots: the running gag. Two such gags revolve around Sonia's habitual tardiness and her wearing inexpensive—and sometimes "exotic"—clothes that she buys after the play the clothes were used in closes. The first gag becomes boring almost immediately. The second, more original gag retains its cleverness awhile, but is milked dry.

The scene in Act Two in which Vernon and Sonia decide to separate is flawed structurally. What had upset Vernon greatly during the earlier stages in his relationship with Sonia were Leon's intrusions in Sonia's life and Sonia's aggressiveness. Yet when Vernon tells Sonia they should break up, the problems caused by Leon are abruptly dismissed. Sonia announces that her preoccupation with Leon is a thing of the past, and Vernon accepts her statement. Sonia's aggressiveness is played down, too. Suddenly the stumbling block in their romance is Vernon's inability to decide whether he wants Sonia to be strictly his professional partner, his lover, or both. What makes the tardy appearance of this lovers' problem even more unconvincing is that previously Vernon told Sonia at length how happy he was living and working with her in the apartment they shared.

Nonetheless, the book Simon contributed to the musical does have its virtues. Many of the jokes, although not up to Simon's best material, are quite funny. Several individual scenes work exceptionally well. In Scene One Simon sets up a stereotyped situation and then pulls a switch or two on it. He draws humor out of the stock predicament of a relatively unknown artist, Sonia, meeting a successful artist, Vernon, and being more than a little nervous. Gradually, however, Vernon learns that Sonia is not all that intimidated. She none too subtly intimates to him that his range as a composer is too limited and timid. Also, after he somewhat patronizingly reassures her about the quality of her lyrics for the music he has just written, she tells him the first eight bars of his melody need work. Their date at the nightclub contains an amusing twist which keeps the sentiment from becoming too sticky. During their tender conversation, each of them forgets about the other whenever the band plays a song he or she helped create.

The final two scenes in Act One are also particularly charming. Once more, romantic clichés are punctured. When Vernon and Sonia settle down in their "cozy lovers' cottage" for the weekend, it turns out that Sonia, arriving first, has mixed up the address of the cottage Vernon reserved for their tryst and has forced her way into the wrong cottage. Later, just before Vernon prepares to join Sonia in bed, she tells him to bring some "pistachio nuts for afterwards."[1] Finally, unlike the endings of most musical comedies, all the lovers' problems do not disappear in the last scene of *They're Playing Our Song*. In fact, when Sonia cites one still-potent problem, Vernon can say no more than, "We'll deal with it" (112). Only then do Sonia and he embrace while the music swells. Even in this romantic musical, then, Simon does not revert to the completely rosy happy endings he provided in his first plays.

The play has one other distinctly creditable attribute: the characterization of Sonia. Unlike Alan Baker's sweetheart Connie in *Come Blow Your Horn,* Sonia does not worry about remaining a virgin until she marries. Nor does she believe she must choose between love and a career. And she certainly does not cater continuously to the man she loves. She is, in fact, so bold she increases Vernon's lack of self-confidence. In Scene Four, the focus on her relationship with Leon emphasizes more facets of her interesting personality. She by no means plays Leon off against Vernon. She truly is no longer in love with Leon, but she is not a person who flushes a man out of her life when their love affair ends. Earlier, she told Vernon that she "doesn't give up easily on relationships" (17), a trait which makes her final reunion with Vernon entirely plausible.

When Vernon and Sonia discuss the creative process, Sonia offers the more interesting viewpoint. Via these exchanges, Simon offers his final contribution to the musical's ultimate success. Vernon, like Diana Nichols in *California Suite* and Elliot Garfield in *The Goodbye Girl,* is an artist lacking in self-confidence. He has also evolved an artistic credo that duplicates Diana's. He believes that fears and neuroses are stimulating sources of creativity and, therefore, should not be seriously tampered with, even though they intensify an artist's lack of self-confidence. Sonia, like Elliot, does not bow down to this belief. Elliot does not let his fears and doubts dominate him; he strives—successfully—to gain more self-confidence; and he suffers no loss of artistic ability in the process of doing so. Sonia has no gnawing neuroses; she is so loaded with confidence she is almost overbearing; and her career is soaring. Indeed, although she admits to Vernon that her private life is sometimes messy, she maintains a businesslike orderliness when it comes to her professional work. Thus, just as Simon in *Chapter Two* stopped suggesting that guilt feelings were always a positive moral force one should cater to, so in *The Goodbye Girl* and *They're Playing Our Song,* he stops suggesting that, in order to create superior artistic works, the artist must surrender himself to his fears and neuroses.

I Ought to Be in Pictures

Like *They're Playing Our Song,* Simon's next full-length comedy, *I Ought to Be in Pictures,* also deals with an insecure male artist and an aggressive young woman. Libby Tucker arrives unannounced at the West Hollywood bungalow where her father, Herb, lives and works. She has not seen him since he left and later divorced Libby's mother, Blanche, sixteen years ago. Steffy, whom Herb has been dating for two years, is the first to greet Libby. When alone with Libby, Herb is so nervous and guilt-ridden over not having kept in contact with her or her brother Robby, he snaps at her until she storms angrily out of the bungalow. Prodded by Steffy, Herb goes after Libby, takes her to dinner, and invites her to stay with him. He explains that Blanche and he were severely incompatible, and that he divorced her rather than have Libby and Robby grow up in a home filled with hostility.

In two weeks' time, Libby transforms the bungalow into very attractive living quarters. Aware that Herb's career is in a decline, she has encouraged him to resume writing; earlier in the day, she wished him good luck as he left to present his latest material at a movie studio meeting. When Herb returns home, Libby learns that, suffering a loss of nerve, Herb went to the race track instead of to the meeting. Deeply disappointed, she leaves for her nighttime job without telling him where she works or what time she will be back. Herb, worried about Libby, gives Steffy very little attention. Steffy asks him to make a deeper commitment to her, and Herb bluntly refuses to do so.

By waiting up until Libby returns home, Herb finds out that she parks the cars of people attending Beverly Hills parties and, in the process, tries to make contacts with show-business celebrities. Because a co-worker is making sexual acdvances to her, Libby asks Herb about what he feels while having sex. She describes her mother's physical frustrations and coldness and, beginning to cry, confesses her hunger for and fear of physical affection. Herb holds her in his arms, giving her the warm parental love she has never had. A few days later Libby, having decided she does not want a career in movies, announces she is heading back east. She telephones her mother about her decision and inveigles Herb into talking to Robby and Blanche. Herb tentatively agrees that Robby can visit him next summer. After Libby leaves, Steffy, who came to say goodbye to Libby, asks Herb to join her for the rest of the day. He turns down her offer, declaring he is going to start working seriously on a script. As the play ends, Steffy suggests that Herb and she could get together some other time; Herb accepts the idea.

The moment Libby arrives at the bungalow in Scene One Steffy senses that Libby is going to trigger changes in Steffy's relationship with Herb and in Herb's relationship with Libby, Robby, and Blanche. Herb, characteristically, refuses to confront this possibility—even when Steffy remarks, "Nothing stays the way it is. . . . It moves on and there's not a damn thing you or I can do about it."[2] The catalyst of the change, Libby, is the most interesting character in the play.

Deeply scarred by living in a broken home for sixteen years, Libby loves and sympathizes with her husband-abandoned mother. Through the years she perceived that something vital inside her mother died when Herb left home, and that her mother tried to compensate for the loss of adult companionship by focusing all her love on her children. Libby, however, does not want to be loved as a substitute for someone else. Nor does she seek to be loved exclusively. She wants to share the warmth of love with many people. She loved her wise, now-dead grandmother. She loves her mother and brother, and seeks love from her father. But she does not want to shove Steffy out of her father's life and gain all his affection. On the contrary, she prods Herb to admire and love Steffy more. She also cajoles Herb into making congenial remarks she can include in the letter she writes her mother. Later, she succeeds in luring Herb into a telephone conversation with Blanche and Robby.

Libby is interesting in other ways. She is well aware of her shortcomings. She cannot accept Herb's opinion she is good-looking; she considers herself too fat. At one point, she expresses her disappointment about not being as attractive as she dreamed and hoped she would be. Conscious of both her physical and nonphysical inadequacies, she is apprehensive every time a boy pays serious attention to her. Yet, although she admits she is scared from the minute she wakes up every morning, she is not hobbled by her fears or her knowledge of her shortcomings. She still pushes forward. She pursues an acting career. Although she gradually realizes that Herb is floundering both professionally and in his personal life, and that he does not want her to make any demands on him, she fights to establish a close relationship with him. She is also able to articulate her unhappiness about the lack of parental love in her life, and, in so doing, to gain love from her father.

Unfortunately, however, Libby is not a continuously believable character. About twenty, Libby is supposed to be on the brink of adult maturity. She crosses the country in a fairly conservative manner, taking public transportation most of the way; and, having had all the schooling she desires, she reasonably enough has begun to think seriously about a career for herself. Yet at times her brashness, her insensitive bluntness, and her view of life make her seem not twenty, but thirteen years old. For a "hip" young woman from Brooklyn, she is too naive. She arrives at the bungalow with an incredibly dreamy, idealistic mental picture of the Hollywood writer. Someone as smart as she is would have researched Herb's professional credits and become aware of his lack of them in recent years. Equally unrealistic is the long amount of time it takes her to figure out her father's present plight. One glance at Herb's bungalow should have told her everything she needed to know about his situation. Nor would a bright urban twenty-year-old with average looks and no acting experience be so silly as to believe she could break into the movies by writing her name on a card and leaving the card on the windshield of a celebrity's car. Finally, as Walter Kerr pointed out, it is impossible to accept that Libby is still so ignorant and inexperienced about sex.[3]

Yet the weaknesses in Simon's presentation of Libby are dwarfed by the problems residing in his delineations of his other two characters. When Steffy attempts to nurture Herb's affection for her and to pry him away from his fear of making another commitment to a woman, she captures the audience's attention. All too often, however, Steffy does not actually participate in the drama. Sometimes, she simply directs Herb and Libby to each other, or she furnishes them with an opportunity to speak their thoughts aloud to someone. At still other times, she is merely the mouthpiece by which Simon tells the audience how to interpret the actions of the other two characters. Steffy proclaims, "I'm no psychiatrist," while providing precisely the kind of insights a psychiatrist might offer. She tells Herb, for instance, that Libby did not write to him about coming west because she was afraid Herb would tell her not to come. Steffy continues, "She wants to know who you are. She wants to know why you let her grow up without you." Still analyzing Libby, she observes, "Maybe saying 'Get me into the movies' is just another way of saying 'Let me back into your life.'" Then she adds, "Maybe she just wants you to do something for her to prove that you never really stopped caring" (32). Later, Steffy analyzes Herb. She hints to him that he nurses the two trees on his property in lieu of his not having helped raise his two children.

At another point, Steffy remarks to Herb, "To love someone is to be scared every minute of your life" (61). The fear of making a commitment of love is the theme around which the play revolves. Libby embodies basic conflicts. She is frightened, yet courageous; cocky, yet insecure; demanding, yet giving. She is afraid of love, yet fights to gain Herb's love. As Steffy stated, Libby's desire to become an actress is primarily her way of trying to reenter Herb's life. Herb, by comparison, is boringly bland. He is, in fact, a deliberately bland person, for above all else he wants to avoid any kind of confrontation, either with others or with himself. Most of his emotions have been so successfully suppressed for so long they exert no vital influence in his life. Hence, there is little conflict within him. He is always simply unsure of himself, fearful, and hesitant. Except, to some extent, with Libby near the end of her visit, Herb makes only tentative demands on other people; when they ask for something in return, he retreats from the relationship.

Lacking any dynamic conflicting emotional pulls, Herb could be as interesting a character as Libby is only if he scrutinized his fears and doubts. He does not do so. He is no longer doing quality writing. He is barely able to put any words on paper. Yet he never attempts to confront this major problem. At the end of the play, he speaks of doing some serious writing centered on "an old idea" that came to him "sixteen years ago" (96). His comment implies that his writer's block stems from his leaving his wife and children, and that now, because he is once more in contact with Libby, Robby, and Blanche, he will be able to write again. This implication, coming out of the blue and not developed any further, seems merely a way of providing the play with a happy ending; it does not offer any fruitful insight into Herb's psyche. Herb was, after all, quite a successful writer during much of the sixteen-year period that followed his leaving his family. If the emotional upheaval bred by his breakup with Blanche led to a writer's block, the block took an awfully long time in solidifying. So, too, Simon has dramatized in other plays that it is not inevitable that an artist riddled with anxiety and doubts will be creatively sterile. Turmoil can nurture superior artistic performances. In sum, neither Herb nor the audience learns anything significant about Herb's personality from his writing difficulties.

Herb states repeatedly that he is afraid of attachments to other people because he is afraid of the possibility of ensuing unattachments. But he never scrutinizes this fear. During the past sixteen years, he married two more times. Both marriages were fiascos that ended in divorce. One would like to know why Herb married the particularly horrendous—(at least in his opinion)—females he did. Was he subconsciously punishing himself for having left his first wife and his children? Not nearly enough information about Blanche and about her marital years with Herb is given to supply an answer to that question. Also, why has Herb never acknowledged that his three failures at marriage are not so much the cause of his consuming fears and doubts as they are the result of them?

Herb never tries to learn why. Indeed, that he failed miserably three times in marriage indicates that he has never learned anything fundamental about himself.

Herb does finally allow himself to respond emotionally to Libby. He worries about her. He comforts her when, describing her unhappiness, she breaks down sobbing. If, however, this is supposed to signify a psychological breakthrough for Herb, one remains unconvinced. Herb's actions seem only a whim of the moment. He has broken through his fears and emotional coldness, but only as the result of a moment's rush of mood. He has not changed in any essential way. He has not learned anything more about himself than Evy Meara in *The Gingerbread Lady* learned about herself while at the sanitarium. What is much more dramatically convincing is that Herb still refuses to commit himself emotionally to Steffy; for this act, though failing to reveal what makes Herb tick, is at least consistent with his pattern of behavior.

After presenting in various plays and films several artists whose traits included a lack of self-confidence, in *I Ought to Be in Pictures* Simon directly focuses on an artist whose whole personality centers on this one trait. Yet, having done so, Simon has little to say about such a person beyond hinting vaguely that an early-in-life trauma in this person's life bred self-doubts and an incapacity to love. Herb is as lackluster as Vernon Gersch in *They're Playing Our Song*—and less witty. He is repeatedly overshadowed by Libby. But Libby, acting at times like someone twenty and at times like someone thirteen, is not always a convincing character. Because *I Ought to Be in Pictures* does not have a compelling plot, its success depends on its presentation of its three characters. The flaws in the depiction of these characters renders the play an inferior piece of work.

Seems Like Old Times

Seems Like Old Times received more praise from film critics than most of Simon's earlier original screenplays did. The fast-moving story begins with two criminals kidnapping Nick, played by Chevy Chase, from his cabin and forcing him to help them to rob a bank. A bank camera takes a picture of Nick, and a copy of the picture ends up on the District Attorney's desk. Ira (Charles Grodin), the District Attorney, is married to Nick's former wife, Glenda (Goldie Hawn), a lawyer specializing in defending the downtrodden. When Nick is turned loose by the criminals, he is afraid to go to the police because he has already served a jail sentence resulting from his attempt to research an article on drug dealers. He heads for Glenda. Although Ira and Glenda are hosting a big party when he arrives at their home, Nick manages to tell Glenda his plight. The next morning, Glenda goes to Nick, now hiding in the room above the garage, and says she will defend him. When Ira enters the room, Nick hides under a cot.

Nick finally leaves, but reappears at Glenda's home several hours before Ira and Glenda are to entertain the Governor and others for dinner. Aurora, the cook, has to go to the hospital, so Glenda—"aided" by Nick—stays home to prepare the dinner meal. After telling her he will surrender, Nick tries to rekindle his romance with Glenda, who tells him she is "content" with Ira. Nick serves the meal, and Ira, enraged, has a fistfight with him back in the kitchen. In an ensuing courtroom scene, Nick is cleared of all charges. That evening, Ira and Glenda decide to drive away from everything and everybody. When they hit a bad rainstorm, however, the car crashes through a fence, and Ira breaks his leg. Seeking help, Glenda sees a light in a cabin window and knocks on the cabin door. Nick opens the door, and Glenda smiles.

While some films based on Simon's screenplays have been underrated, *Seems Like Old Times* is overrated. The plot premise is woefully weak. *The Talk of the Town*, a 1942 comedy which clearly served as the inspiration for Simon's script, offered a sound plot involving a male fugitive from justice, a male representative of the judicial system, and an unmarried woman attracted to both men—all of them holed up in the same house. In *Seems Like Old Times*, because it is so obvious that Nick is forced to do what the criminals tell him to do, it is impossible to believe that the police would declare Nick a bank robber. Similarly, Nick's motivation for not going to the police—the matter of his previous conviction—is all very hazy, hence unconvincing. Finally, that Nick, disheveled and unshaven, wanders around for days without any trouble in the posh neighborhood where Ira and Glenda live is implausible and distracting.

As the plot evolves, other major problems arise. It is never made clear why Glenda and Nick split up. There are vague indications that Nick is supposed to represent an undisciplined although engaging side of Glenda's personality which she is trying to smother. Nick, however, is not engaging or charming; he is rarely anything but lumpish. Ira, on the other hand, is apparently intended to be the stodgy type of character Ralph Bellamy played in such films as *His Girl Friday*. Actually, Ira is handsomer, cleverer, and often funnier than Nick. Thus it is hard to accept that Glenda would seriously consider chucking her attractive present husband in order to return to her less appealing first husband. Yet the praise given the film is by no means totally unwarranted. Not since *The Heartbreak Kid* has Simon written a screenplay so effectively geared to be a movie and not a series of scenes in which people talk. *Seems Like Old Times* is a *motion* picture from the opening sequence when Nick wrestles with the two criminals right through to the conclusion when Ira's car splits a fence rail and Glenda runs toward the cabin light. Nick's funniest moment in the movie is entirely visual. His attempt, while hiding under the cot, to cope with Ira's shoe pinning his finger to the floor is hilarious. In this scene, the usually phlegmatic Nick offers a variety of facial expressions—revealing pain, stoicism, helplessness, and frustration. He also fights the temptation to use his free hand to pound angrily on Ira's foot.

The long climactic sequence, the dinner party for the Governor, provides the best sustained humor in the movie. Before she leaves for the hospital, Aurora mangles the English language delightfully. Chester, a tipsy butler, contributes clever quips. In the kitchen, Glenda and Nick engage in rapid exchanges of dialogue as lively as the banter in the 1930s screwball comedies. Equally fine are Ira's and Glenda's efforts, despite the mounting chaos of the meal, to hold everything together in order to keep Ira's political future a bright one. The Governor's determination to keep cool amid the clamor is comic icing on the cake.

The film, however, has no clear point to make. The only statement it comes close to making is one that echoes the point of view in those 1930s movies Simon is so fond of. Glenda ultimately focuses her attention on the man she loves, not on her career. In so doing, she resembles Paula, who, in *The Goodbye Girl,* is quite ready to abandon her career for the man she loves—just as Connie is in Simon's very first play, *Come Blow Your Horn.* The decision made by all three women states Simon's belief that a person's individuality is not as important as the social unit (be it a couple, a family, or whatever).

Another problem in *Seems Like Old Times* is that Glenda, Nick, and Ira are as poorly developed a trio of characters as the main characters in *The Star-Spangled Girl.* So, too, the mercurial quality of the plot persists right to the end. The wacky courtroom scene is reminiscent of earlier film comedies in which everything is straightened out even as the judge becomes more and more bewildered. On the other hand, the film's last episode is much too trumped up. Ira and Glenda's sudden impulse to drive through the pouring rain to nowhere in particular is unconvincing. The whole sequence is constructed solely to allow Glenda to end up with Nick, a dubious prize.

Fools

No other play by Simon had nearly as short a run on Broadway as *Fools*. Its plot, taking place at no specific time, is also quite different from anything else Simon had written for the theater. At the start of the play, Leon Tolchinsky, a young college-educated man, wends his way toward the village of Kulyenchikov in response to an advertisement stating that Doctor and Mrs. Zubritsky want a tutor for their daughter Sophia. Leon soon learns that, because years earlier a member of the unpoular Yousevitch family was refused the hand of a Zubritsky maiden, the Yousevitches laid the curse of stupidity on all the villagers. When Sophia's parents prove as dumb as all the other villagers Leon met before reaching their house, he becomes exasperated. Then he sees Sophia and immediately falls in love with her. That evening, Sophia comes out on her balcony, and Leon discovers that his deepening love for her is matched by her love for him.

Although warned that if he remains in town twenty-four hours he, too, will be inflicted with stupidity, Leon continues to tutor Sophia. He also finds out that if a Zubritsky and a Yousevitch marry, the curse will be lifted, and that Gregor Yousevitch has been courting Sophia. Later that day, Leon appears to have been struck dumb by the curse. He only faked being dumb, however, in order to try to show the villagers that the curse works only through the power of suggestion—the villagers, feeling guilty about the wrong done to the Yousevitch family, allow themselves to be convinced they must be stupid. Leon decides to take even more positive action. He asks Gregor Yousevitch to adopt him so that Leon can marry Sophia and "break the curse." After the wedding ceremony begins, Gregor announces he will not, after all, permit Leon to use the Yousevitch name. Gregor pressures the Zubritskys into agreeing to let him marry Sophia. Now it is Leon's turn to stop the ceremony. He pretends that a postcard he received reports that his uncle, before he died, changed the family name to Yousevitch. For a third time, the wedding ceremony begins. The moment Leon and Sophia are married an explosion occurs, and when all the people get back up on their feet, they are no longer stupid. A dance celebrating everyone's good fortune takes place.

It would logically follow that, given the poorest reception of any play written by Simon, *Fools* should be Simon's poorest play. It is not. It is clearly better than *The Star-Spangled Girl* and *God's Favorite*. More than that, the best scenes in *Fools* are as funny as—or funnier than—those in *The Good Doctor* and all the musicals Simon wrote except, perhaps, *Little*

Me. The long scene in Act One when Leon talks with Doctor and Mrs. Zubritsky and then, too, with Sophia is thoroughly engaging. The jokes revolving around the parents' stupidity are varied, keeping the humor fresh. Several jokes involve different kinds of wordplay. Others are visual in emphasis. Still others evolve from bright-eyed Sophia's delightful simplicity, innocence, and budding fondness for her handsome, dedicated tutor. Gradually, more and more of the scene's humor emerges from the characters and the basic situation—two parents who want their daughter educated and married and two young people who are falling in love.

The Romeo-and-Juliet interlude that soon follows creates the fairytale atmosphere Simon had hoped would permeate the whole play. The proceedings are not only funny, but charming—the charm emanating from the spontaneous, child-pure Sophia and the love-struck Leon. This balcony scene also contains more tenderness and simple affection than Simon's plays and movies usually offer. Yet the scene never sinks into oversweet sentimentality. In Act Two, Sophia, responding to Leon's ardor and tutoring, becomes more vibrant and joyfully aggressive. The climactic wedding scene supplies much superior humor. Several of the villagers are at their comic best. Gregor's villainy—and his enjoyment at being a villain—adds to the entertainment. The scene turns poignant when it appears that the two young lovers will not be permitted to wed; and Leon's quick-witted way of saving the day for true love is engaging. The wedding dance caps the happy-ending spirit of the story.

Although Simon used a plot and set of characters far removed from his plays' usual milieu, *Fools* dramatizes several of Simon's basic beliefs. Once again, as he did in *Chapter Two* and *I Ought to Be in Pictures,* Simon attacks the negative, hobbling effect of guilt feelings. *Fools* implies that people, docilely using others' invalid standards, judge themselves too harshly. Through Sophia's achievements in response to Leon's tutoring, Simon also suggests that people would have more respect for themselves if they did not take their everyday accomplishments for granted. Gaining self-respect, people would seek love more confidently and be able to nurture and share love. Here, too, are beliefs concerning self-confidence, love, and the power of positive thinking that link *Fools* thematically not only with *Chapter Two* and *I Ought to Be in Pictures,* but with *The Goodbye Girl* and *They're Playing Our Song.*

The reason the play is not a success is that the good things in it are isolated entities. What occurs between the play's best moments is never better than mediocre. Quite uncharacteristically for a Simon play, *Fools* takes a long time reaching its first flow of humor. First, Leon meets a shepherd in the outskirts of Kulyenchikov and, later, several of the villagers; and these scenes are only sporadically amusing. Their sole point, namely, to show that the villagers are stupid, is established in thirty seconds. Examples of the villagers' stupidity appear throughout the play and become monotonously repetitious. The villagers lack any interesting individuality, for their one dominant trait is their stupidity. So, too, some of the characters' wisecracks jar with the unsophisticated never-never-land atmosphere Simon tried to establish.

Fools is atypical of Simon's work in its dearth of interesting characters and its ultimately heavy emphasis on plot. This uniqueness would cause no problem if the plot were a clever one. Unfortunately, that is not the case. The plot is much too slow in unfolding during Act One. Then Simon *stuffs* the second act with plot. The plot-turns come too rapidly and are unconvincing. For instance, the idea that the villagers' stupidity stems from the power of suggestion is dramatized—then dropped. Leon's pretending to be dim-witted becomes pointless because he abruptly pursues other means of breaking the curse. The play is also weakened by Simon's failure to develop the character of Gregor Yousevitch. Until his last appearance, Gregor is one of the most lackluster villains ever presented in a fairy tale or fable. He is not comically spiteful. He is not comically anything. The story depends on Gregor to supply some conflict, and he only does so midway through the second half of the play.

It is too bad that *Fools* is a weak effort, for it represents one of Simon's most radical creative experiments to date, and the failure of that experiment is hardly likely to spur Simon toward more such ventures in the future. Because through the years Simon has been written off as someone who "manufactures" the same type of comedy over and over, it is equally unfortunate that he won so little praise for at least attempting something new in *Fools*. Ignoring his courage, some critics made a point of chastising Simon for not sticking to the successful style and milieu he had utilized in earlier years.

Only When I Laugh

When Simon wrote the film-script based on *The Gingerbread Lady*, he did not give the script the same title the play had—and with good reason. For the first time, Simon radically altered the material he transferred from one of his stage plays to the screen. *Only When I Laugh* utilizes considerably less than 50 percent of the material that *The Gingerbread Lady* presented to theatergoers. Georgia Hines, the main character in *Only When I Laugh,* had in the past the same problems concerning alcohol and obesity that Evy Meara had in *The Gingerbread Lady.* Unlike Evy, however, Georgia does not spend her time at the sanitarium making a pass at her psychiatrist. As the film opens, Georgia, played by Marsha Mason, is earnestly trying to discover and explain to her doctor the causes of the problems that led to her latest—and, she hopes, her last—stay in a sanitarium. While Evy returned to her New York apartment and waited for something to trigger her next bout with the bottle, Georgia comes back home legitimately hopeful that she can conquer her self-destructive tendencies. Consequently, after Georgia gossips with her friends Jimmy (James Coco), a homosexual actor, and Toby (Joan Hackett), an aging married woman, she hesitates only briefly before acquiescing to her daughter Polly's desire to come live with her. After Polly (Kristy McNichol) moves in, Georgia is also much more willing to discuss her past with her offspring than Evy was.

Another major difference between *The Gingerbread Lady* and *Only When I Laugh* centers on the lovers linked with Evy and with Georgia. When Evy's lover Lou Tanner reappeared after Evy's stay in the sanitarium, he was as narcissistic and immature as ever. David, Georgia's ex-lover, although as selfish as Lou, has altered his life considerably during Georgia's absence. He wrote a play based on their tumultuous relationship and found a producer for the play. Now, aware that Georgia still loves him, David successfully manipulates her into accepting the lead in the play. He states that he has a new girl friend, but he never discourages Georgia from believing she can rekindle his love for her.

For a while, Georgia's life is on the upswing. Polly and she have good times together. Meanwhile, Jimmy gains a major role in a play rehearsing for an Off-Broadway opening, and Toby plans a birthday party for herself. Then, a stunned Toby tells Georgia that her husband is leaving her. Jimmy is fired from the cast. Worst of all, Georgia's straightforward attempt to regain David's love leads to her humiliation, for David uses the occasion to introduce her to his current girl friend. Georgia attempts to phone her psychiatrist, but a colleague is covering for him and is no help at all to Georgia. That night, at Toby's party Georgia downs several drinks, ignoring Polly's plea that she stop drinking. Later that evening, a man Georgia talks with in a bar follows her outside and forces her to have sex with him.

Bruised and with a black eye, Georgia spends the night at Toby's apartment. Although distraught about her own problems, Toby will not allow Georgia to berate herself. Toby tells Georgia how jealous she is of Georgia's talents and admirable traits. Nonetheless, the next day Georgia, filled with self-contempt, pressures Polly into moving out. Although Polly declares she still loves Georgia, Georgia refuses to promise to meet Polly and Georgia's ex-husband, Polly's father, for lunch that afternoon. After Polly leaves, Georgia confides to Jimmy how astonished she was to learn that Polly loves her so much. Jimmy tells her that everyone loves her because she is a special person—quite superior to the image she has of herself. Then he expresses his satisfaction that Georgia, Toby, and he are now free to resume the way of life they shared before Georgia's last stay at the sanitarium. Jolted by the prospect of resuming such a sterile, self-destructive existence, Georgia resolves more firmly than ever before to strive for a better life and joins her ex-husband and a delighted Polly at a restaurant for lunch.

A synopsis of *Only When I Laugh* clearly indicates the great number of alterations Simon made in changing *The Gingerbread Lady* into a movie. The quality of the changes is a mixed bag. The characterization of Toby, for example, is diluted in the film. She, like Jimmy, serves mainly to present the witty, but basically negative, life-style that Georgia ultimately spurns. Toby's other important function is to lecture Georgia about how foolishly self-deprecating Georgia is—while in the play Evy lectured Toby and helped straighten out Toby's life. On the other hand, Jimmy in the film version is a somewhat less self-centered, more insightful, and more interesting person. Yet what he relishes most of all is meeting with others, such as Toby and Georgia, who have failed in life and making bitchy comments about everyone else.

Simon tried hard to make Polly a more vivid character in the film than she was on stage. He was only partially successful. In the film, Polly does have more of a life independent of her relationship with Georgia. She has boyfriends and boyfriend problems. She has a good friend in Heidi, a classmate. Both girls are in a high-school play, and have even more fun trying to "fix Georgia up" with one of their teachers.

Nonetheless, Polly remains a flaw in the story. She is still too good to be true, too unselfish. She is also stolidly unflappable; even when she becomes angry, she never loses control of herself. Her desire to live with her mother appears motivated not so much by love as by a grim stubbornness. Polly's attempt to instigate a relationship between her teacher and her mother rings true both as a harebrained teenage scheme and as wish-fulfillment. But her attempt, while out shopping with Georgia, to arrange a double date for Georgia and herself with two young college boys is so silly, self-defeating, and out of character as to be impossible to believe. Another lame sequence comes after Polly sees Georgia drinking at Toby's party. Polly obtains a bottle of liquor and proceeds to taste "demon rum" apparently for the first time in her seventeen-or-more years of life, which seems quite implausible. Although Polly vomits repeatedly, she has no hangover the next day; and, as opposed to what happened between Evy and her daughter, Polly does not lead Georgia into discussing the latter's alcohol problem.

Once or twice on earlier occasions, Georgia, while talking seriously with Polly, does probe her past in order to try simultaneously to understand her past behavior and to correct Polly's misinterpretations of Georgia's past actions concerning their relationship. During most of the time she is with her daughter, however, Georgia is inane. She reverts from a woman to a scatterbrained kid. She scolds Polly for setting up the meeting between Georgia and the high-school teacher, but neither Polly nor Georgia takes the scolding seriously. When they flirt with the two college boys, Georgia appears even more silly.

Yet Georgia is an entirely different person in her relationship with her ex-lover David. Engaged in telephone conversations or face-to-face encounters with David, she is a thoroughly intriguing woman. David quickens the adult traits in Georgia's personality, rekindles her love for him—and outsmarts her at every turn. The presentation of subtle David is another one of Simon's superb character delineations. David is in love only with himself. When he sees the billboard advertising his play, he is mesmerized by it. Aware of Georgia's low estimation of herself, David repeatedly entices her into believing he—talented, handsome, and intelligent—is on the verge of resurrecting their love affair. Upon her return home from the sanitarium, he teases her with suspense concerning why she wants to see her again. When, to her deep disappointment, Georgia discovers David wants her in his play primarily because he thinks her presence in it will increase the chances for the play's success, David starts telling Georgia how great he thinks she is as an actress and as a person. He calculatingly feeds her desperate hunger for praise.

Simon's portrait of David is flawless. His portrait of Georgia, although flawed, is more gripping. Beyond the faulty relationship between Polly and Georgia, the main flaw in Georgia's characterization is that Simon attempted to graft some of Evy's traits and actions onto Georgia. Fortunately, Simon did not try to present Georgia as someone quite as vehemently self-destructive as Evy. As a result, the movie audience grants Simon the film's happy ending, while the theater audience could never buy the happy ending offered in *The Gingerbread Lady*. Yet it is hard to believe that Georgia was even as self-destructive as the audience is told repeatedly she once was. Lou Tanner, Evy's lover, certainly could have helped drive Evy to drink and to a mental collapse. On the other hand, although one hears about David's past wildness, no evidence of it ever appears. Thus, one can easily believe that David could make Georgia tense and miserable, but not that he could lead her to seek oblivion in a whiskey bottle and have a nervous breakdown.

Evy possessed strong elemental drives for food, alcohol, and sex and was often crude, even vulgar. The movie audience is told that Georgia has the same drives, but all she does is stuff herself with junk food on one occasion. At other times, she leaves food on her plate. Polly's use of swear words is supposed to reflect Georgia's influence, but actually Georgia swears very little. Willfully irresponsible, Evy had no control over her life and was fatalistically certain that disaster would strike again. Her going on another bender was inevitable. Georgia's bender, despite the bad day she has had, seems arbitrary and at least somewhat unconvincing. Her taking a drink or two appears motivated merely by a need to calm herself, not by a desire to obliterate reality from her consciousness. Indeed, when she is back in her apartment with Jimmy after the party, she is sleepily tranquil. Her sudden urge to go out and drink in a bar is even more unconvincing than her mini-bender at Toby's party.

Georgia is not as powerful or fascinating a character as Evy. Nonetheless, when Simon stops tacking Evy's traits and actions onto Georgia, he presents his film audience with a very interesting woman. Georgia, unlike Evy, is not driven by primitive physical needs but by an intense desire for love. Unlike Evy, Georgia never blames other people or Life for anything. She blames herself. Georgia's affair with David is a misery for her because she has given her heart to a cold, calculating egotist, yet cannot stop herself from admiring him for the strength he has and that she thinks she does not possess. She loves Jimmy and Toby, but they, too, are ultimately too self-centered to respond in kind. Furthermore Jimmy, a homosexual, could never give Georgia the type of love she yearns for, a love including not only sex but a home and family. Consequently, Jimmy cannot dissuade her from believing she does not deserve love. Nor can Georgia gain the kind of love she wants from a stage career or from doctrinaire guidance counseling. Georgia's furious rejection of the impersonal platitudes she receives over the telephone from the colleague substituting for her psychiatrist provides what is perhaps the single most compelling moment in the film.

What is particularly exciting about Georgia is that, because she has so much to offer other people, one wonders if she will stop offering it primarily to selfish people such as David. One is gripped with the hope that Georgia will learn what she is on the brink of sensing when the movie begins, namely, that she is not a hopeless bungler and, therefore, can find love and happiness. The happy ending is plausible and satisfying because—prompted by the praise she receives from Toby and Jimmy, and by Polly's love for her, and by her realization that she does not want to spend the rest of her life with self-pitying, self-destructive people— Georgia finally does believe that the love she desires is there for the taking. She can, for a start, accept and bask in Polly's love for her.

Interestingly enough, *Only When I Laugh,* a story containing far fewer funny lines and much more sadness than almost anything else Simon has written, became one of his most popular creative efforts, while his preceding effort, the lighthearted *Fools,* was quickly dismissed by the public and the critics. Yet the two works emphasize identical points. Both dramatize how wrong it is that many people judge themselves so harshly and dismiss their best qualities and their achievements as insignificant. Both stress that if more people felt the self-respect and self-confidence they are validly entitled to feel, they would find the fulfilling love relationships they yearn for. But although *Fools* is an interesting and somewhat underrated experiment, it is not of outstanding quality. *Only When I Laugh,* despite its flaws, is one of the most absorbing pieces of work that Simon has written.

Chapter Twelve
One of Our Finest Writers of Comedy

Because Neil Simon's creative efforts have been part of our cultural scene for over twenty years, many people consider themselves knowledgeable about his work. These people would compare Simon to a sausage grinder turning out the same pleasing "product" over and over again. The "product" is a play or movie realistic in style and featuring New Yorkers who spout a lot of funny lines.

Actually, Simon's writings are more varied both in style and in quality than most people realize. Simon's film-scripts, for instance, have been quite mercurial in quality. For several years Simon did not commit himself wholeheartedly to his film assignments. When adapting one of his plays, he was preoccupied with transferring the material to the screen as intact as possible. He usually succeeded in achieving this limited goal, and his success constituted his punishment. Most of these film adaptations can be rated no better than satisfactory; some are pedestrian. One exceptionally good early film is *The Odd Couple,* but then, in this case, the basic material was exceptionally good to begin with.

Simon's lack of commitment also derived from his preferring to work in a Broadway theater rather than on a Hollywood soundstage. This led to his not fighting as fiercely in Hollywood to get his production ideas incorporated in his films. Then, too, for many years he simply did not have as much power in the film world as he did in New York. Even when he did fight various artistic battles, he often lost. This was particularly true, for instance, with *After the Fox.* It was true, too, although not to the same degree, concerning the first American film projects in which he participated.

Simon had to decide whether or not he was going to increase the amount of time and energy he devoted to the filming of his scripts. When he began working with such men as producer Ray Stark and director Herbert Ross, and began writing scripts his wife, Marsha Mason, starred in, Simon did intensify his degree of involvement in movie-making. This led to the deserved success accorded such films as *The Sunshine Boys, California Suite,* and *The Goodbye Girl.* Simon took an even bolder step with *Only When I Laugh.* He became a coproducer and created a film that ranks with his finest adaptations and original screenplays.

Still, the whole story of the quality of Simon's filmwork is not tied solely to his decision to write more carefully for the screen and to take a more active part in the process of filming his scripts. Several movies that were based on material Simon prepared specifically for Hollywood and that were filmed with great care proved to be inferior films. The problem here was simply that Simon's scripts were fault-ridden. *The Out-of-Towners* is shallow and repetitious and features an unpleasant, unfunny "comic" character. Both *Murder by Death* and *The Cheap Detective* ultimately drown in all kinds of problems, including belabored parodies and dull plots. *Seems Like Old Times* is hobbled by a continuously implausible plot and a male hero who is supposed to be—but fails to be—more attractive than his romantic rival.

Yet even the bouncy, charming *The Goodbye Girl,* a success both at the box office and artistically, illustrates another shortcoming in Simon's film work. Simon has remained too enamored of the kinds of movies he saw while growing up. He has never seriously utilized any of the successful experiments in cinematic form developed by other filmmakers in recent decades. His fascination with detective films and Bogart films caused him to lose his artistic objectivity when he wrote *Murder by Death* and *The Cheap Detective.* He was too convinced his parodies of those earlier films provided surefire laughs. *Seems Like Old Times* is a comparatively better achievement, and *The Goodbye Girl* considerably better. Nevertheless, both films are essentially little more than updated imitations of comedies typical of earlier decades.

Of the film-scripts Simon has written that were not adaptations of his plays, *The Heartbreak Kid* is by far the most interesting. Although based on a Bruce Jay Friedman short story, Simon's version of the material shows more originality than any of his original screenplays do. The plot premise—a man on his honeymoon finds his bride's coarse "little habits" intolerable and, simultaneously, meets the living embodiment of his Dream Girl—is developed with skill and wit. The film builds to an absorbing climax and intriguing denouement. The main characters are vividly individualized, yet become meaningful and memorable archetypes.

Concerning theatrical endeavors, it is still not valid to describe Simon as a writer who grinds out the same kind of product year after year. He has written definitively simple situation comedies such as *Come Blow Your Horn,* and, with *The Odd Couple,* a situation comedy featuring two complex characters. He has written an outstanding domestic comedy, *Barefoot in the Park.* He not only includes a wacky vaudeville skit within *The Sunshine Boys,* but deftly integrates this skit's speech patterns and point of view in all the scenes preceding and following the skit. In *The Good Doctor,* using Chekhov stories as sources, Simon offers adaptations in styles that range from broad farce to subtle understatement. *God's Favorite* is a modern rendition of the Book of Job. *Fools* combines the style and plot of a fairy tale with a fable's moral message. Again employing a range of styles, *Plaza Suite* and *California Suite* present excellent one-act plays. Finally, Simon has written the books for a lighthearted satirical musical, *Little Me*; a sentimental-comedy musical, *Sweet Charity*; a sophisticated, biting satirical musical, *Promises, Promises*; and a romantic-comedy musical, *They're Playing Our Song.*

Because of the four musicals Simon helped create, and because of some of the comedies he created, it is inaccurate to say that all of Simon's successful theater work is contained in his comedies about New Yorkers. Nor is it true that all of Simon's finest characters are New Yorkers. To be precise, one would have to say that most of Simon's finest characters are urban-dwelling Americans. Yet some of Simon's entertaining characters do not fit into even this larger category. Diana and Sidney Nichols, in *California Suite,* are English. In *Little Me,* old Mr. Pinchley, Otto Schnitzler, and Prince Cherny—delightful characters all—also remain outside the broader definition of a typical Simon character. The same holds true for the amusing characters in both *The Good Doctor* and *Fools.*

Variety—not sameness—in style is, however, only one of several basic characteristics of Simon's plays. Like *Born Yesterday, The Rose Tattoo,* and *Mister Roberts,* Simon's mature theater work combines comedy with moments of poignance and insight. Examples abound. In *The Odd Couple,* Oscar Madison and Felix Ungar, although hilarious to see and listen to, demonstrate how destructive a selfish person can be. *Promises, Promises* dramatizes how Chuck Baxter and Fran Kubelik, who think they can manipulate people at no cost to themselves, learn that others, more shrewd and calculating, manipulate them and make them pay heavily for their proud schemes. The exchanges between Bill and Hannah Warren in *California Suite* reveal how easy it is to misjudge who is the strong person and who is the weak, and to fail to perceive that although two people talk at length about one topic, their views on that topic merely reflect thoughts and feelings rooted in more fundamental aspects of their lives. *Plaza Suite, The Sunshine Boys,* and *Chapter Two* also do a superb job of fusing the comic and the insightful. Another recurring feature in Simon's plays is the humor itself. It might seem facetious to state that Simon's plays are consistently—at times, dazzlingly—funny. But much too often this primary component of his work is taken for granted. It is not true that all of Simon's hit shows consist of clusters of funny one-liners. Yet even if it were true, it would be no small accomplishment. Precious few people can write any kind of funny lines. Thomas Meehan has written, "An ability to write comedy is an innate talent that can't be taught, learned, bought, or even rationally explained. You either have it or you don't." Meehan also stated, "One mustn't overlook the fact that Simon writes funnier jokes than almost anyone else around."[1] In the 1961–1981 period, Simon's success in creating page after page of laugh-provoking dialogue is unmatched by any other playwright's efforts. Indeed, very few playwrights have matched his achievement during any twenty-year period.

Simon admitted that early in his playwriting career he was guilty on occasion of stuffing a one-liner into some character's mouth. Quickly, though, he weeded out such lines from the drafts of his newer plays; and, soon, all the humorous conversation emanated from the plot and characters. If, then, while discussing Simon's work chronologically, one gradually stops quoting funny lines, it is not because they dwindle in number. There are as many funny lines in the conversations between Diana and Sidney Nichols as there are in those between Corie and Paul Bratter in *Barefoot in the Park.* In the best later plays, however, the richness of character delineations and related matters demands that a discussion of these works concentrate on quotations pertaining to character and theme.

Simon does, on the other hand, sometimes have problems with his plays' structure. *Fools,* which gives little attention to characterizations and, instead, focuses on its fairy-tale story, is woefully weak in structure. The plot barely moves forward in the first part of the play; in the remainder, it has far too many twists and turns. *Come Blow Your Horn* is repetitive in construction and too contrived at times. *Barefoot in the Park* dramatizes a tension between Corie and her mother, then suddenly drops the whole matter. Happy endings that are not entirely convincing occur in several plays, including *The Odd Couple, I Ought to Be in Pictures,* and, most clearly of all, *The Gingerbread Lady.* A few plays, however, are exceptionally sound in structure. For example, *Chapter Two* deftly intertwines its complicated major and minor plots. In *California Suite,* the lurking fundamental problem in the relationship between Diana and Sidney Nichols is adroitly set up step by step until it finally declares itself—a declaration causing a major crisis in the Nicholses' marriage. *The Sunshine Boys* has an airtight structure.

With regard to character delineation, Simon has no peers among contemporary comedy playwrights. Other writers have created vivid characters—but not in the sheer abundance Simon has. Even if one leaves aside the captivating broad comedy characters found in such plays as *The Good Doctor, Plaza Suite,* and *California Suite,* plus the liveliest characters in all the musicals, there are still numerous compelling characters, major and minor, in the more realistic comedies. To cite only one play's excellently sketched minor characters, there are the feckless musician Lou Tanner and the homosexual actor Jimmy Perry in *The Gingerbread Lady* (with the latter being even more interesting in the film version). Concerning major characters, the overbearing Mr. Baker in *Come Blow Your Horn* and, especially, the hard-drinking Evy Meara in *The Gingerbread Lady* are so sharply etched they do not allow Simon to conclude the plays they appear in with as smooth an upbeat ending as he wished. Although they appear only in one-act plays or in one act of a play, Sam and Karen Nash, Jesse Kiplinger, and Muriel Tate in *Plaza Suite,* Elaine Navazio and Jeanette Fisher in *Last of the Red-Hot Lovers,* Hannah and Bill Warren, and Diana and Sidney Nichols are all superbly depicted individuals. Despite some faulty strokes on Simon's part, he still offers his audience engaging characters in the enigmatic Al Lewis in *The Sunshine Boys* and in Paul, Corie, and Corie's mother. The former play also presents one of Simon's finest creations, Willie Clark. All four participants in *Chapter Two* can be added to the roster of outstanding characters, as can Barney Cashman, the main character in *Last of the Red-Hot Lovers.* Finally, capping the list are two characters who are now as much a part of American cultural folklore as Huck Finn and Babbitt—*The Odd Couple*'s Oscar Madison and Felix Ungar.

Another dominant feature of Simon's work is his outlook on life. As is true for all other outstanding writers of comedy, Simon humorously dramatizes his serious basic beliefs. Through his characters, he suggests that the individual should choose to remain within the social network. No Simon hero or heroine makes the ultimate Romantic gesture of thumbing his or her nose at society. Buddy Baker, the young man in *Come Blow Your Horn* who wants to be a writer, is still willing to continue working in his father's business. Despite pressuring Paul to maintain a vibrant and somewhat carefree private life, Corie will help Paul further his lawyer-career. Even the "revolutionaries" in *The Star-Spangled Girl* want to reform, not blow up the social system. Simon's emphasis in these early plays on the desirability of working within society remains undiminished in his later works. In *Last of the Red-Hot Lovers,* for instance, Barney Cashman's attempts to break free of society's conventions render him comic, not heroic. In all his plays from *Come Blow Your Horn* to his most recent work, Simon honors the ultimate symbol of the social network: the family unit. In order to preserve her marriage and to keep her children happy, Millie Michaels, in *California Suite,* accepts even the humiliation of talking to her children over the telephone while the arm of the call girl her husband has had sex with lies in Millie's lap.

This stress not on the primacy of the individual, but on the primary importance of society has triggered negative reactions in several critics. Some critics, assuming that Simon's "old-fashioned" beliefs constitute no beliefs at all, declare his work flimsy and superficial. Most members of the audience, however, are delighted to find Simon upholding their own beliefs. Simon's point of view, though, does not arise simply out of a desire to pander to the beliefs of the "moral majority." Simon opts for society because he sincerely believes that human beings are frail creatures who will be less vulnerable to attack and more likely to thrive if they seek the nourishment society provides.

By no coincidence, then, two virtues Simon stresses are moderation and fidelity. To function well within society, one must compromise. To compromise, one must be mature enough willingly to embody moderation. Too much ego or self-love, found in Oscar Madison and Felix Ungar, for example, is destructive. Some of the wives and sweethearts in Simon's writings, including Jennie Malone in *Chapter Two* and Sonia Walsk in *They're Playing Our Song,* are spunky individuals. Yet ultimately each of them, even Sonia, bends to some degree to the man in her life in order to preserve the relationship she has with him. Rarely, if ever, do those who pursue sexual infidelity gain happiness. Sam Nash's affair with his secretary leads him not so much to romance as to bewilderment. In *Chapter Two,* Leo Schneider's extramarital sexual triumphs leave him still unsatisfied, while Faye Medwick's "affair" with Leo leads her back to her husband. Barney Cashman, after three straight rendezvous that prove fiascos, ends up phoning his wife for a date.

In Simon's eyes, divorce is never a victory. Herb Tucker in *I Ought to Be in Pictures* and Jesse Kiplinger are just two of several characters whose divorces have not brought them happiness. Jennie Malone admits that her ex-husband was by no means entirely to blame for their divorce. She blundered, too, and hopes now she has gained enough insight into herself from the failure of her first marriage to prevent her second marriage from heading to the divorce courts.

Although the moral beliefs the Simon advocates are "old-fashioned" ones, his view of human experience is not blithely sentimental. The happy endings in his best plays are often only minimally happy. Chuck Baxter and Fran Kubelik finally get their lives on the right track, but they have been deeply scarred in the effort and are more than a little gun-shy emotionally. Equally scarred are the Nicholses and George Schneider and his wife, Jennie. Hannah and Bill Warren have gained merely a brief respite; both know that, within hours after they part, they will be confronted with problems as serious as the problem they have just solved. Herb Tucker is so scarred he panics at the thought of making what Simon stresses in several plays people must make—a serious commitment to other human beings. Mimsey Hubley in *Plaza Suite* panics, too, on her wedding day, although she, unlike Herb, does finally dare to make such a commitment.

Simon also acknowledges the complexity of human experience. *Last of the Red-Hot Lovers* shows that guilt feelings can lead to moral conduct that, in turn, brings happiness and a sense of relief. But both *Chapter Two* and *Fools* demonstrate that guilt feelings can be negative, destructive forces. Simon celebrates love and tenderness in *Promises, Promises,* yet in that same play points out that people must be tough in order to defend the love they feel and share. The meetings between Muriel Tate and Jesse Kiplinger in *Plaza Suite* and between the Warrens in *California Suite* portray how a simple course of action can be ladened with a bewildering complexity of conflicting motivations. Furthermore, Simon reveals in play after play how greatly the fear of aging and dying complicates every human being's life.

Simon emphasizes the need for honesty, yet he demonstrates that honesty does not always provide a solution to troubles. Honesty can be more destructive than creative. Karen and Sam Nash's discussion "clears the air" between them, but their frankness renders a formerly difficult marital situation impossible. Evy Meara's keen perception of reality reinforces, if not causes, her self-destructive alcoholism and promiscuity. An honest eye's exposure of the ridiculous is sometimes painful. The Nicholses, much to Diana's chagrin, recognize the absurdity involved in the Academy Awards. More grimly, Jennie realizes that her husband, George, pays closest attention to her needs not when she is all-giving, but when she lashes out angrily at him. Elaine Navazio perceives the essential starkness of human existence so vividly she can only continue to function by narrowing her life to a series of short, intense sensuous gratifications.

Finally, however, Simon does suggest that, if risked, honesty can ultimately prove constructive. Corie and Paul, Diana and Sidney, Jennie and George—many of Simon's couples—engage in bluntly honest exchanges and, as a result, pave the way toward better, stronger relationships. Both Barney Cashman and Faye Medwick feel relieved and legitimately optimistic after they admit to themselves that they are simply not cut out to be "swingers." Willie Clark gains at least a modicum of peace when he accepts the fact he is now an old man.

Walter Kerr has stated, "Whenever a playwright manages to be hilariously funny all night long . . . he is in immediate danger of being condescended to."[2] Because Americans have always tended to underrate writers who make them laugh, Neil Simon's accomplishments have not gained as much serious critical praise as they deserve. His best comedies contain not only a host of funny lines, but numerous memorable characters and an incisively dramatized set of beliefs that are not without merit. Simon is, in fact, one of the finest writers of comedy in American literary history.

Notes and References

Chapter One

1. Tom Prideaux, "He Loves to Kill Them," *Life,* 9 April 1965, p. 39.
2. "The Human Comedian," *Newsweek,* 9 January 1967, p. 70.
3. Maria Karagianis, "World's Richest Playwright Stars as Harvard Professor," *Boston Globe,* 1 March 1979, "Calendar," p. 11.
4. Paul D. Zimmerman, "Neil Simon: Up from Success," *Newsweek,* 2 February 1970, p. 54.
5. Lawrence Linderman, "Playboy Interview: Neil Simon," *Playboy* 26 (February 1979):68.
6. Neil Simon, "Notes from the Playwright," in Edythe M. McGovern, *Neil Simon: A Critical Study* (New York, 1979), p. 3.
7. Alan Levy, "Doc Smith's R_x for Comedy," *New York Times Magazine,* 7 March 1965, pp. 42–43.
8. All page references are to *Come Blow Your Horn* in *The Comedy of Neil Simon* (New York, 1971), p. 28.
9. All page references are to *Little Me* in *The Collected Plays of Neil Simon, Vol. II* (New York, 1979), p. 35.
10. Howard Taubman, "Slickness, Not Charm," *New York Times,* 2 December 1962, Section 2, p. 1.
11. All page references are to *Barefoot in the Park* in *The Comedy of Neil Simon,* p. 111.
12. McGovern, *Neil Simon,* p. 27.
13. John McCarten, "Light and Lovely," *New Yorker,* 2 November 1963, p. 93.
14. McGovern, *Neil Simon,* p. 33.

Chapter Two

1. Linderman, "Playboy Interview," p. 74.
2. All page references are to *The Odd Couple* in *The Comedy of Neil Simon,* pp. 220–21.
3. Simon, "Notes from the Playwright," pp. 3–4.
4. Walter Kerr, "What Simon Says," *New York Times Magazine,* 22 March 1970, p. 14.
5. Howard Taubman, review of *The Odd Couple, New York Times,* 11 March 1965, p. 36.
6. Simon, "Notes from the Playwright," p. 3.

Chapter Three

1. All page references are to *Sweet Charity,* book by Neil Simon, music by Cy Coleman, lyrics by Dorothy Fields (New York, 1966), p. 113.

2. Joan Barthel, "Life for Simon—Not That Simple," *New York Times,* 25 February 1968, Section 2, p. 9.

3. All page references are to *The Star-Spangled Girl* in *The Comedy of Neil Simon,* p. 306.

4. Clive Hirschhorn, "Make 'em Laugh," *Plays and Players* 24 (September 1977):13.

5. Linderman, "Playboy Interview," p. 76.

6. Brendan Gill, "Particeps Criminis," *New Yorker,* 7 January 1967, p. 89.

7. Bosley Crowther, review of *After the Fox, New York Times,* 24 December 1966, p. 11.

8. "The Human Comedian," p. 70.

9. "Dialogue on Film," *American Film* 3 (March 1978):36.

10. Barthel, "Life for Simon," p. 9.

11. All page references are to *Promises, Promises* in *The Comedy of Neil Simon,* p. 395.

Chapter Four

1. Zimmerman, "Neil Simon," pp. 52, 55.

2. All page references are to *Plaza Suite* in *The Comedy of Neil Simon,* p. 497.

3. McGovern, *Neil Simon,* p. 58.

4. Walter Kerr, "Simon's Funny—Don't Laugh," *New York Times,* 25 February 1968, Section 2, p. 5.

Chapter Five

1. All page references are to *Last of the Red-Hot Lovers* in *The Comedy of Neil Simon,* p. 585.

2. McGovern, *Neil Simon,* p. 77.

Chapter Six

1. Linderman, "Playboy Interview," p. 58.

2. Richard Meryman, "When the Funniest Writer in American Tried to Be Serious," *Life,* 7 May 1971, p. 64.

3. All page references are to *The Gingerbread Lady* in *The Collected Plays of Neil Simon, Vol. II,* p. 153.

4. Stanley Kauffmann, "Last of the Red-Hot Writers," *New Republic,* 16 January 1971, p. 22.

5. Otis L. Guernsey, Jr. ed., *Playwrights Lyricists Composers on Theater* (New York: Dodd, Mead and Company, 1974), p. 235.

6. Linderman, "Playboy Interview," p. 74.

7. Ibid.

8. All page references are to *The Prisoner of Second Avenue* in *The Collected Plays of Neil Simon, Vol. II*, p. 231.

9. Simon, "Notes from the Playwright," p. 4.

10. Brendan Gill, "Laughing When It Hurts," *New Yorker*, 20 November 1971, p. 111.

11. John Corry, "Why Broadway's Fastest Writer Cannot Slow Down," *New York Times*, 5 April 1981, Section 2, p. 1.

12. Jack Kroll, "Exploring Lewis and Clark," *Newsweek*, 1 January 1973, p. 52.

13. Pauline Kael, *When the Lights Go Down* (New York: Holt, Rinehart and Winston, 1975), p. 77.

14. Simon, "Notes from the Playwright," p. 4.

Chapter Seven

1. "Dialogue on Film," p. 36.

2. Arthur Knight, "What's So Damned Funny?" *Saturday Review*, 13 June 1970, p. 26.

3. Roger Greenspun, review of *The Out-of-Towners*, *New York Times*, 29 May 1970, p. 14.

4. Stephen Farber, "You See Yourself in 'Heartbreak,'" *New York Times*, 18 February 1973, Section 2, p. 1.

5. Vincent Canby, review of *The Heartbreak Kid*, *New York Times*, 18 December 1972, p. 56.

Chapter Eight

1. Mel Gussow, "Simon's New Play Is a 'Change of Pace,'" *New York Times*, 27 November 1973, p. 48.

2. Linderman, "Playboy Interview," p. 58.

3. Gussow, "Simon's New Play," p. 48.

4. All page references are to *The Good Doctor* in *The Collected Plays of Neil Simon, Vol. II*, p. 393.

5. McGovern, *Neil Simon*, p. 129.

6. Jack Kroll, "What's Up, Doc?" *Newsweek*, 10 December 1973, p. 118.

7. All page references are to *God's Favorite* in *The Collected Plays of Neil Simon, Vol. II*, p. 493.

8. Linderman, "Playboy Interview," p. 76.

9. Rowland Barber, "A Californian Named Neil Simon Heads for Broadway," *New York Times*, 6 June 1976, Section 2, p. 5.

10. All page references are to *California Suite* in *The Collected Plays of Neil Simon, Vol. II*, p. 552.

11. Linderman, "Playboy Interview," p. 74.

Chapter Nine

1. All page references are to *Chapter Two* in *The Collected Plays of Neil Simon, Vol. II*, p. 649.

2. Richard Eder, "For Neil Simon, It's 'Chapter Two,'" *New York Times*, 5 December 1977, p. 52.

Chapter Ten

1. Linderman, "Playboy Interview," p. 68.

2. Judith Crist, "A Cheer for Hollywood," *Saturday Review*, 11 November 1975, p. 31.

3. Molly Haskell, review of *The Cheap Detective*, *New York*, 10 July 1978, p. 75.

4. Linderman, "Playboy Interview," p. 60.

Chapter Eleven

1. All page references are to *They're Playing Our Song*, book by Neil Simon, music by Marvin Hamlisch, lyrics by Carole Bayer Sager (New York, 1979), p. 67.

2. All page references are to *I Ought to Be in Pictures* (New York, 1980), p. 65.

3. Walter Kerr, review of *I Ought to Be in Pictures*, *New York Times*, 4 April 1980, Section C, p. 3.

Chapter Twelve

1. Thomas Meehan, "The Unreal, Hilarious World of Neil Simon," *Horizon*, January 1978, p. 74.

2. Walter Kerr, "Simon's Funny—Don't Laugh," p. 1.

Selected Bibliography

PRIMARY SOURCES

1. Plays
The Collected Plays of Neil Simon, Vol. II. New York: Random House, 1979.
The Comedy of Neil Simon. New York: Random House, 1971.
I Ought to Be in Pictures. New York: Random House, 1980.
Sweet Charity. Book by Neil Simon, music by Cy Coleman, lyrics by Dorothy Fields. New York: Random House, 1966.
They're Playing Our Song. Book by Neil Simon, music by Marvin Hamlisch, lyrics by Carole Bayer Sager. New York: Random House, 1979.

2. Essay
"Notes from the Playwright." In: *Neil Simon: A Critical Study.* By Edythe M. McGovern. New York: Frederick Ungar, 1979.

SECONDARY SOURCES

Anon. "Dialogue on Film." *American Film* 3 (March 1978):33–48. In addition to supplying information on several of Simon's plays, this interview contains a wealth of material on Simon's film work, especially *Barefoot in the Park, The Heartbreak Kid,* and *The Goodbye Girl.*
Farber, Stephen. "You See Yourself in 'Heartbreak.'" *New York Times,* 18 February 1973, Section 2, p. 1. An exceptionally penetrating analysis of the film based on Simon's best screenplay, *The Heartbreak Kid.*
Hirschhorn, Clive. "Make 'em Laugh." *Plays and Players* 24 (September 1977):12–15. An interview in which Simon offers an incisive analysis of *The Star-Spangled Girl* and of the pressures of success.
Kerr, Walter. "What Simon Says." *New York Times Magazine,* 22 March 1970, pp. 6, 12, 14, 16. One of the first articles to cite and discuss the serious elements in Simon's stage comedies, Kerr's essay is particularly insightful concerning *The Odd Couple* and *Plaza Suite.*

Linderman, Lawrence. "Playboy Interview: Neil Simon." *Playboy* 26 (February 1979):58, 60, 62, 66, 68, 73–76, 78. So far, the best interview that Simon has given. In it, Simon analyzes his development as a playwright from his first play to *They're Playing Our Song*; he also straightforwardly discusses his two marriages, *The Goodbye Girl,* and the casting of several of his movies.

McGovern, Edythe M. *Neil Simon: A Critical Study.* New York: Frederick Ungar, 1979. The first full-length study of Simon's stage comedies through *Chapter Two,* this underrated book offers both detailed synopses of the plays and many insights into individual plays by Simon and into the canon of Simon's comedies.

Meehan, Thomas. "The Unreal, Hilarious World of Neil Simon." *Horizon* 21 (January 1978):70–74. An intelligent, if somewhat patronizing outline of Simon's basic beliefs and attitudes and of the makeup of the audience that enjoys Simon's urban-centered plays.

Meryman, Richard. "When the Funniest Writer in America Tried to Be Serious." *Life,* 7 May 1971, pp. 60B–60D, 64, 66–69, 71, 73, 75, 77, 79–80, 83. This absorbing account of the history (starting with the first rehearsals) of the Broadway production of *The Gingerbread Lady* also offers a variety of comments on Simon by his brother, Danny, and his friends and professional associates regarding Simon's career and personality.

Monaco, James. "The Sunshine Boys Make Movies: Neil Simon, Mel Brooks, Woody Allen." In: *American Film Now.* New York: Oxford University Press, 1979, pp. 232–48. Although he devotes only three pages to Simon's film work and is too quick to grant others' adverse criticisms of that work, Monaco points out Simon's lack of control over movies made from his screenplays; praises such films as *The Sunshine Boys, The Heartbreak Kid,* and *California Suite*; and quite rightly stresses the major contributions such directors as Elaine May and Herbert Ross made to films scripted by Simon.

Zimmerman, Paul D. "Neil Simon: Up from Success." *Newsweek,* 2 February 1970, pp. 52–56. In this article focusing on Simon's career through the opening of *Last of the Red-Hot Lovers,* Simon talks about his childhood, his early years as a comedy writer, and his desire, after the success of his first plays, to portray more complex characters within plays utilizing a more sophisticated structure.

Index

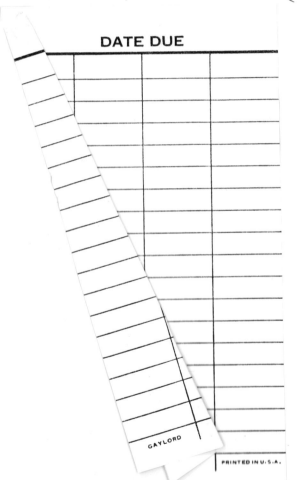

DATE DUE

GAYLORD

PRINTED IN U.S.A.